A First Book
of Bridge Problems

Patrick O'Connor

MASTER POINT PRESS • TORONTO, CANADA

P9-DVZ-504

Master Point Press
331 Douglas Ave.
Toronto, Ontario, Canada
M5M 1H2   (416)781-0351

Email: info@masterpointpress.com

Websites: www.masterpointpress.com
                       www.teachbridge.com
                       www.bridgeblogging.com
                       www.ebooksbridge.com

Library and Archives Canada Cataloguing in Publication

O'Connor, Patrick, 1941-
          A first book of bridge problems / Patrick O'Connor.

Issued also in electronic formats.
ISBN 978-1-897106-83-9

          1. Contract bridge. I. Title.

GV1282.3.O36 2011   795.41'5   C2011-906226-7

Editor	Ray Lee
Copy editor/interior format	Sally Sparrow
Cover and interior design	Olena S. Sullivan/New Mediatrix

1 2 3 4 5 6 7   15 14 13 12 11
PRINTED IN CANADA

Acknowledgements

I am extremely grateful to Kay, my wife and bridge partner, for her tireless editing and many ideas for improvement and for giving me the benefit of her consummate teaching skills. I also appreciate her patience with my spending time on bridge problem composition instead of other activities such as gardening and painting the house.

I would also like to thank Suzie Fitzadam and Beth Haggerty for their comments and suggestions, which were most helpful.

I am grateful to Ray and Linda Lee of Master Point Press for their editing and suggestions for improvement of the book.

Contents

Introduction

This is not a 'how to play bridge' book. It is a book of problems for novices who have completed an introductory course on bridge and may be already playing in club duplicates or supervised sessions. Experienced players recognize certain standard situations without having to think about it, whereas a novice will spend a lot of mental effort trying to work them out. The book will help the novice player to develop their skill at recognizing these situations.

The book comprises fifty problems, presented in approximate order of difficulty. The idea is to present bridge hands as you, the reader, would encounter them playing at the table. Each deal has a single theme. Unlike a textbook, where topics are introduced systematically, this book will give you no clue as to what type of play is required.

Planning the play at the first trick is emphasized in the book. Good players always pause after dummy comes down to plan the hand. Weak players tend to rush in without thinking. To this end there is a brief initial chapter entitled 'Planning the Hand'.

South is always the declarer in these problems. Most of the time you are declarer but sometimes you are a defender sitting East or West. The bidding system is very standard and is summarized on p. 111. The bidding is not usually relevant to the play of the hand but it is given as a reinforcement of standard bidding. If you play another system it doesn't affect the problems, which are all about the play. Where points are mentioned, they are high-card points — you may add points for distribution if you wish using whatever method you were taught.

Each problem is presented with two of the four hands shown. There are several question points within the problem where the reader can attempt a solution or read further. The full deal is shown overleaf with the solution. The key point of each problem is spelled out at the end.

On p. 113 you will find a glossary of common bridge terms in case you are not familiar with any of the jargon in the book.

Finally, there are themes and key points for each of the problems listed on pp. 115-119. These enable you to look up a theme and find the problem(s) in which it occurs, or to see the key points of each problem.

I hope you enjoy the book.

Planning the Hand

Planning the play in notrump

These are the steps to planning the play in a notrump contract:

- Count your winners
- Decide whether you need to develop tricks
- Don't be afraid to give up the lead
- In general, establish your extra tricks before cashing sure tricks
- Plan your entries

An example of counting your winners:

```
        ♠ K Q 9 8 2
        ♡ J 10 9
        ♢ 7 6 4
        ♣ A 3
        ┌──────────┐
        └──────────┘
        ♠ A 4 3
        ♡ A 7 4 3
        ♢ K Q J 10
        ♣ K 10
```

South is in 3NT. West leads the ♣Q.

Look at both hands, suit by suit. In spades, you have the ace, king and queen that could win you three separate tricks. You might make two more tricks with the nine and the eight but this is not certain so you can't count them as winners. They may have to be developed. In hearts you have one immediate winner — the ace. In diamonds you have no winners! Tricky here — you won't have any certain winners until you have lost a trick to the ace but after that the remaining high cards will be winners. In clubs you have two winners. So you have six winners and must develop three more to make 3NT.

How can you develop three more tricks? Looking at spades, the opponents have five between them. About two thirds of the time one person will have three spades and the other two. Roughly a quarter of the time they split 4-1, but a 5-0 split is pretty uncommon. It doesn't hurt to remember these numbers. If they split 3-2 this will give you five spade tricks but still only eight winners in total.

The best bet is the diamond suit. As mentioned above, once you knock out the ◇A you will have three winners, which is just what you need. So you plan to lead a diamond immediately when you get in and keep leading them until the ace appears. This will give you nine tricks. Then if the spades break 3-2 you will get two extra tricks as a bonus.

Planning the play in a suit contract

These are the steps in planning the play in a suit contract:

- Count your losers
- Decide whether you need to develop tricks
- Consider trumping losers in the short hand
- Draw trumps first unless you need to dispose of losers beforehand
- Don't be afraid to give up the lead
- Plan your entries

An example of counting your losers:

♠ J 10 2
♡ K 10 9 5
◇ A 8 4 2
♣ 7 3
[　　　]
♠ A K Q 4 3
♡ A 7 4
◇ 7 6
♣ A J 10

South is in 4♠. West leads the ◇K.

Find the hand with more trumps — in this case it is South. It is known as the long trump hand. Consider only losers in the long hand. In spades the ace, king and queen will take tricks and the jack and ten in the short hand will take care of the four and three in the long hand, so no losers in spades. In hearts the ace will take a trick and the seven and four are losers, but the king will take care of one of them so you only have one loser. In diamonds the seven and six are losers but the ace will take care of one of them so you only have one loser. In clubs you have the ace plus two losers, neither of which can be covered by the short hand. So you have four losers — one in hearts, one in diamonds and two in clubs and you need to eliminate one of them to make your contract.

There are thirteen tricks in a deal. Take your four losers from thirteen and you get nine. That is, you expect to take nine tricks in 4♠. But you need ten, so you have to eliminate one of your losers.

Can you trump a loser in the short hand? Yes — since you have three clubs in the long hand, South, and only two in the short hand, North, you could trump one in the short hand. The next thing to consider is whether you can safely draw trumps first. If there is no reason to delay, you should always draw trumps first. In this case if you draw trumps there will be none left in dummy to trump a club. So you plan to lead the ♣A and then another club. When you regain the lead, you will able to draw a round or two of trumps leaving one in dummy and then trump your losing club. This will give you ten tricks and your contract.

There are other possibilities here but trumping a loser in dummy is the best bet to eliminate a loser.

PROBLEM 1

You are South, declarer in 1NT.

```
        ♠ A K 9
        ♡ 4 3 2
        ◇ 4 3 2
        ♣ 5 4 3 2

            N
        W       E
            S

        ♠ 4 3 2
        ♡ A K 9
        ◇ A K 9
        ♣ Q J 10 6
```

West	North	East	South
			1NT
all pass			

You open 1NT (15-17 points) with your balanced hand. North, who also has a balanced hand and needs at least 8 points to invite to game, passes.

West leads the ♠Q. How will you make seven tricks?

Analysis

The first thing to do in notrump is to count your winners. You have two each in spades, hearts and diamonds. You need one more trick to make your contract.

West has probably led the ♠Q from a four-card or longer suit headed by the ♠QJ10, with the plan of taking several spade tricks after your ace and king have been knocked out. There are no extra tricks in spades available for you.

What is the best way to proceed?

SOLUTION 1

```
                    ♠ A K 9
                    ♡ 4 3 2
                    ◇ 4 3 2
                    ♣ 5 4 3 2
  ♠ Q J 10 6 5                        ♠ 8 7
  ♡ 7 6 5          ┌─────────┐        ♡ Q J 10 8
  ◇ Q J            │    N    │        ◇ 10 8 7 6 5
  ♣ A K 9          │ W     E │        ♣ 8 7
                   │    S    │
                   └─────────┘
                    ♠ 4 3 2
                    ♡ A K 9
                    ◇ A K 9
                    ♣ Q J 10 6
```

No matter what you do in hearts or diamonds there is no way to make a third trick in either suit. Look at the diamond suit — if you play the ace and king, the queen and jack will drop but East will control the third round with the ten. In hearts you can lead small ones from dummy towards your ♡AK9 but East will play an honor each time so your nine will never win a trick.

The only suit that will yield a seventh trick is clubs, and all you have to do is knock out the opponents' ace and king. You have to lose some tricks in spades, but you can still make your contract if you establish your club suit before you cash the winners in hearts and diamonds.

So win the opening lead with the ♠A in dummy and lead a small club to your ♣Q. West will take the ♣K and probably continue with the ♠J. Take this in dummy with the ♠K and lead another club to your ♣J. West will win this with the ♣A and cash three spade tricks: you will follow suit to the first and discard the ♡9 and ◇9 on the next two. Now your ♣10 and ♣6 will be good, giving you eight tricks.

Key Point

Develop tricks in suits where you hold more cards than the opponents.

PROBLEM 2

You are South playing in 3NT.

```
          ♠ A K 10 8
          ♡ A K 10 7
          ◇ 8 3 2
          ♣ 5 4

              N
          W       E
              S

          ♠ Q J 6
          ♡ Q J 3
          ◇ A J 4
          ♣ A 8 6 2
```

West	North	East	South
			1NT
pass	2♣	pass	2◇
pass	3NT	all pass	

You open 1NT (15-17 points) and partner bids 2♣ (the Stayman convention) to see whether you have a four-card major. You reply 2◇, showing no four-card major. Partner, who has a good hand and doesn't want to miss out on game, bids 3NT.

West leads the ♣K. How do you plan to play the hand?

Analysis

As everyone tells you, it is important to plan the play at Trick 1. In notrump, the first thing to do is to count your winners. You have four in spades, four in hearts and the two minor aces — that's ten tricks.

So what's the problem? Why not start by cashing the nice major aces and kings in dummy?

```
                    ♠ A K 10 8
                    ♡ A K 10 7
                    ◇ 8 3 2
                    ♣ 5 4
    ♠ 9 7 5                              ♠ 4 3 2
    ♡ 4 2            ┌──────────┐        ♡ 9 8 6 5
    ◇ K 10 9         │   N      │        ◇ Q 7 6 5
    ♣ K Q J 7 3      │ W     E  │        ♣ 10 9
                     │   S      │
                     └──────────┘
                    ♠ Q J 6
                    ♡ Q J 3
                    ◇ A J 4
                    ♣ A 8 6 2
```

If you cash the aces and kings of spades and hearts before thinking, you will not be able to take the fourth trick in either major. The third round in either suit will put the lead in your hand with no way to get back to dummy. The suits will be blocked. You will end up with only eight tricks.

The key to unblocking is to cash the winners from the hand with fewer cards in the suit first. So take the opening lead with the ♣A in your hand. Then cash the ♠Q and ♠J before crossing to dummy by playing the six to the ace. Then you can play the ♠K. Play the hearts in a similar fashion and collect your ten tricks.

 Key Point

Play high honors from the short side first to unblock a suit.

PROBLEM 3

You are South, declarer in 4♡.

```
              ♠ 5 2
              ♡ J 9 7 4
              ◇ J 5 2
              ♣ A 10 6 4
```

```
              ♠ A 4 3
              ♡ A K Q 8 6
              ◇ Q 10 3
              ♣ K 3
```

West	North	East	South
		pass	1♡
pass	2♡	pass	4♡
all pass			

You have an 18 HCP hand that you open 1♡. Partner gives you a single raise and you bid game.

West leads the ♠J. How do you plan to play the hand?

Analysis

In a trump contract the first thing to do is to count your losers. You have four losers — two spades and two diamonds.

How will you proceed?

SOLUTION 3

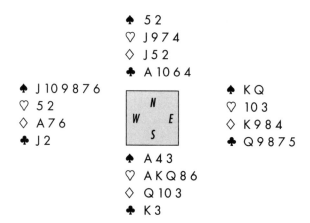

```
                 ♠ 5 2
                 ♡ J 9 7 4
                 ◇ J 5 2
                 ♣ A 10 6 4
♠ J 10 9 8 7 6         ┌─────────┐        ♠ K Q
♡ 5 2                  │    N    │        ♡ 10 3
◇ A 7 6             W  │         │  E     ◇ K 9 8 4
♣ J 2                  │    S    │        ♣ Q 9 8 7 5
                       └─────────┘
                 ♠ A 4 3
                 ♡ A K Q 8 6
                 ◇ Q 10 3
                 ♣ K 3
```

Win the opening lead with the ♠A. You have to lose one spade for sure but you can trump one in dummy. You only need one trump in dummy in order to do this, so you can start drawing trumps. Both defenders follow to two rounds of trumps so now you can play a spade. When you regain the lead you can trump your third spade in dummy. You will inevitably lose two diamond tricks to the ace and king but you will make your contract.

The only danger is if the outstanding trumps are divided 4-0. This will become evident on the first round of trumps. If it happens, stop drawing trumps temporarily and ruff the spade in dummy before resuming the extraction.

The expression 'ruff a loser' means the same as 'trump a loser'. The terms are interchangeable.

Key Point

Where possible, draw trumps before ruffing losers in dummy.

PROBLEM 4

You are South playing in 6NT. Gulp!

```
        ♠ K Q 10
        ♡ K 8 5 4
        ◇ Q 10 9 4
        ♣ K 4

            N
        W       E
            S

        ♠ A 7 5
        ♡ A Q 10
        ◇ A K J
        ♣ Q J 10 8
```

West	North	East	South
			2NT
pass	6NT	all pass	

You open 2NT (20-21 HCP). Partner has a balanced hand with 13 points and knows that the partnership total is 33 or 34 points, so bids 6NT immediately. No messing around!

West leads the ◇8. How do you plan to play the hand?

Analysis

In notrump, the first thing to do is to count your winners. You have three in spades, three in hearts and four in diamonds — that's ten tricks. So how do you go about developing two more tricks?

SOLUTION 4

```
              ♠ K Q 10
              ♡ K 8 5 4
              ◇ Q 10 9 4
              ♣ K 4
♠ J 6 3 2                      ♠ 9 8 4
♡ J 9 7 3        N            ♡ 6 2
◇ 8 3        W       E        ◇ 7 6 5 2
♣ A 7 3          S            ♣ 9 6 5 2
              ♠ A 7 5
              ♡ A Q 10
              ◇ A K J
              ♣ Q J 10 8
```

If you start cashing your top tricks, you can only take ten tricks. By then it will be too late to develop a club trick because West will win the ♣A and take the last two tricks with the ♠J and the ♡J. How sad!

When developing tricks in notrump, it is common to look for long suits with top losers. Here the club suit isn't long, but once you lose a trick to the ace all your other clubs will become winners.

It is important to knock out the ♣A immediately while you still control the other suits. So win the diamond lead in your hand with the ace and lead the ♣8 to the king in dummy. If the ace is not played to this trick, continue with clubs until the ace appears. The only trick you will lose is to the ♣A, so twelve tricks are yours.

Key Point

Develop tricks early while you still have stoppers in the other suits.

PROBLEM 5

You are East. South is declarer in 2♡. Partner leads the ♠K.

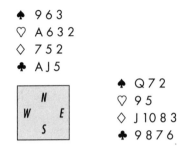

	♠	9 6 3
	♡	A 6 3 2
	◇	7 5 2
	♣	A J 5

♠ Q 7 2
♡ 9 5
◇ J 10 8 3
♣ 9 8 7 6

West	North	East	South
			1♡
dbl	2♡	all pass	

West makes a takeout double of South's 1♡ opening. This shows an opening hand, shortness in the opponent's suit and promises support for any unbid suits. You are obliged to respond to the double even with no points unless your right-hand opponent bids, in which case you can pass if you are weak. North has four hearts and makes a single raise to 2♡, which lets you off the hook. Phew!

West leads the ♠A, which is normally from ♠AK. You play the ♠7 on the ♠K. West continues with the ♠K on which you play the ♠2. This combination of playing a high card followed by a low card on partner's leads is a signal, encouraging partner to continue the suit. Partner continues with the ♠5 to your ♠Q, which wins the trick.

What will you do now?

Analysis

You have no spades left so you have to decide which suit to switch to. There is no point in switching to hearts so the choice is between diamonds and clubs.

Which card will you play?

SOLUTION 5

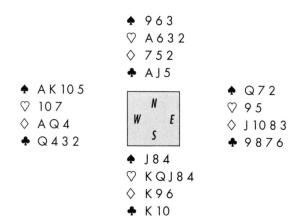

```
              ♠ 9 6 3
              ♡ A 6 3 2
              ◇ 7 5 2
              ♣ A J 5
♠ A K 10 5                         ♠ Q 7 2
♡ 10 7          N                  ♡ 9 5
◇ A Q 4      W     E               ◇ J 10 8 3
♣ Q 4 3 2       S                  ♣ 9 8 7 6
              ♠ J 8 4
              ♡ K Q J 8 4
              ◇ K 9 6
              ♣ K 10
```

When choosing a suit to lead in defense it is a good principle to lead through the strong opponent's hand towards the weak opponent's hand. Dummy has the ♣AJ5, which is strong, but only three small diamonds. If partner has some honors in diamonds they will be sitting over declarer's diamonds, so you can perhaps promote partner's diamonds by leading them.

So the suit to lead is diamonds, but which card should you lead? The answer is the ◇J, because it is the top of a sequence. Looking at all four hands you can see that declarer's ◇K will be trapped between your ◇J10 and partner's ◇AQ. If declarer ducks the ◇J, partner will play low, you will continue with the ◇10. Your side will win three diamond tricks to go with the three spade tricks you already have and the contract will be defeated.

If you return a club instead of a diamond, you will trap partner's ♣Q. Declarer will draw trumps and eventually discard a diamond loser on a winning club from dummy.

Key Point

On defense, when choosing a suit, lead through the strong opponent towards the weak opponent.

PROBLEM 6

You are South, a slightly reluctant declarer in 4♡.

```
            ♠ A K J 9 6
            ♡ Q 2
            ◇ 5 3 2
            ♣ 7 4 2

                  N
              W       E
                  S

            ♠ —
            ♡ J 10 9 8 7 6
            ◇ A K 4
            ♣ A K Q J
```

West	North	East	South
			1♡
pass	1♠	pass	2♣
pass	2♡	pass	4♡
all pass			

You have an unusual hand — six hearts missing the top honors, a void in spades and 17 HCP in the minors. Although you have no card higher than the jack in hearts, it is still the suit to bid. You open 1♡, partner responds 1♠, which is not unexpected, and you bid your second suit, clubs. Partner's spades are not good enough to rebid; expecting you to have five hearts and four clubs for your bidding, partner gives preference to hearts because a 5-2 fit is better than a 4-3 fit as a trump suit. This is enough encouragement for you to go on to game.

West leads the ◇10. What are your thoughts?

Analysis

You have a diamond loser and two in trumps. Unfortunately you will probably not be able to get to dummy to discard your diamond loser on a high spade. The trumps don't look very attractive but at least you have eight of them between your hand and dummy.

Should you start drawing trumps?

SOLUTION 6

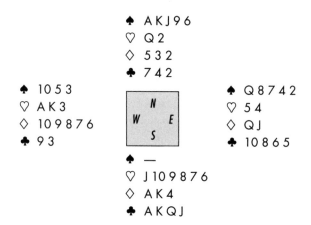

```
                    ♠ A K J 9 6
                    ♡ Q 2
                    ◇ 5 3 2
                    ♣ 7 4 2
   ♠ 10 5 3                          ♠ Q 8 7 4 2
   ♡ A K 3          ┌─────────┐      ♡ 5 4
   ◇ 10 9 8 7 6     │    N    │      ◇ Q J
   ♣ 9 3            │ W     E │      ♣ 10 8 6 5
                    │    S    │
                    └─────────┘
                    ♠ —
                    ♡ J 10 9 8 7 6
                    ◇ A K 4
                    ♣ A K Q J
```

In every suit contract you have to decide whether or not to draw trumps immediately. There are many straightforward deals where you have good tricks to run and you do not have to dispose of losers urgently. In these cases, draw trumps first. This is one of those deals, and the lack of high trumps in your hand and dummy should not deter you.

Win the opening lead with the ◇A in your hand and lead a trump. West will win with the ♡K to deny you access to dummy and then probably continue diamonds. You will win with the ◇K and lead another trump, which West will take with the ♡A. Draw the last trump when you regain the lead and you will make your contract.

Let's look at what might happen if you decide to avoid leading trumps because they look so pathetic. You might decide to attack the club suit. Say you play the ♣A, ♣K and ♣Q. West will ruff the ♣Q with the ♡3. So the defense will end up winning three trumps as well as a diamond.

The point of drawing trumps is to deny the opponents the chance to ruff with their small trumps. So unless there are other considerations such as trumping a loser in dummy or discarding a loser you should draw trumps as soon as possible.

Key Point

Draw trumps early unless you have a good reason for delay, such as trumping a loser in dummy or discarding a loser.

PROBLEM 7

You are South, playing in 4♡.

```
        ♠ 4 3
        ♡ A 7 6 5
        ◇ 10 9 8
        ♣ K Q J 6

            N
        W       E
            S

        ♠ A K 6
        ♡ K J 3 2
        ◇ 7 6 5
        ♣ A 5 3
```

West	North	East	South
			1NT
pass	2♣	pass	2♡
pass	4♡	all pass	

You open 1NT with your balanced 15 HCP. North, looking for a heart fit, bids 2♣, Stayman. You show your four-card heart suit by bidding 2♡ and partner leaps to game.

West leads the ◇K. How do you plan to play the hand?

Analysis

You have three immediate diamond losers and a spade loser that can either be ruffed in dummy or discarded on a club winner. The only problem is how to handle the trump suit.

West takes the ◇K, ◇A and ◇Q and switches to a small spade. Now it is time to tackle trumps. There are five missing hearts, including the queen. Do you play the ace and king to try and drop the queen, or do you play some other way?

```
                    ♠ 4 3
                    ♡ A 7 6 5
                    ◇ 10 9 8
                    ♣ K Q J 6
  ♠ Q 8 7 2                          ♠ J 10 9 5
  ♡ 10 4          ┌──────────┐       ♡ Q 9 8
  ◇ A K Q         │    N     │       ◇ J 4 3 2
  ♣ 9 8 7 2       │ W     E  │       ♣ 10 4
                  │    S     │
                  └──────────┘
                    ♠ A K 6
                    ♡ K J 3 2
                    ◇ 7 6 5
                    ♣ A 5 3
```

When five cards of a suit are missing, the most likely split is 3-2, meaning that West will have three and East two, or vice-versa. If that is so, the queen is more likely to be in the hand with three hearts. If you don't believe this, deal the queen and four small hearts into two piles several times and see how often the queen is in the pile of three.

So the ♡Q is not likely to drop if you cash the ♡A and ♡K. Your only hope is that East has the queen and one or two others. So cross to the ♡A in dummy and then lead the ♡5 towards your hand. If the ♡Q doesn't appear from East, play the ♡J. West plays the ♡10, so you now play the ♡K and drop East's ♡Q. Congratulations, you have successfully finessed against the queen!

This time you make your contract. If West had been dealt the ♡Q, you would have gone down. That's life!

> *With eight cards in a suit missing the queen, finesse.*

PROBLEM 8

You are South. After a simple auction you are declarer in 3NT.

♠ Q 3 2
♡ A K 4
◇ 10 2
♣ Q 9 6 3 2

```
      N
  W       E
      S
```

♠ A K 5
♡ J 7
◇ A 7 4
♣ K J 10 7 4

West	North	East	South
			1NT
pass	3NT	all pass	

You have a balanced hand with 16 points so you open 1NT (15-17 HCP). North has 11 points and no four-card major, so raises you immediately to game.

The lead is the ◇K by West. How do you plan to play the hand?

Analysis

The first thing to do is to count your winners. You have the ♠A, ♠K and ♠Q — that's three. Then the ♡A and ♡K — that's two more, and the ◇A brings the total to six. So you need to find three more tricks. The obvious source of extra tricks is the club suit where you have the king, queen, jack, ten and nine. All you need to do is knock out the ♣A and you will have four club tricks.

Are there any possible problems? Is there anything bad that can happen if you take the ◇A at once and lead a club?

SOLUTION 8

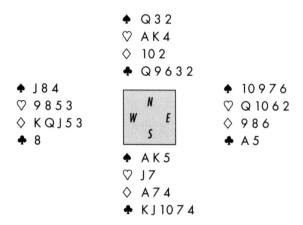

```
                    ♠ Q 3 2
                    ♡ A K 4
                    ◇ 10 2
                    ♣ Q 9 6 3 2
    ♠ J 8 4                           ♠ 10 9 7 6
    ♡ 9 8 5 3          N              ♡ Q 10 6 2
    ◇ K Q J 5 3    W       E          ◇ 9 8 6
    ♣ 8                S              ♣ A 5
                    ♠ A K 5
                    ♡ J 7
                    ◇ A 7 4
                    ♣ K J 10 7 4
```

The danger is that the opponents may be able to take four diamond tricks before you can cash your clubs. The opening lead of the ◇K is most likely from a sequence and it may be from a five-card or longer suit. If it is from a four-card suit there is no problem because each opponent has four cards and they cannot take more than three diamond tricks.

The solution is to let West win the first trick with the ◇K and if diamonds are continued let West win that one as well. Why? Because if West has five diamonds and East has three, East won't have one left to lead to partner after three rounds. Take the third diamond with the ace and then lead a club. Make sure to set up your clubs before cashing your stoppers in the majors. Fortunately, East has the ♣A and is out of diamonds, so you can enjoy your clubs and finish up with ten tricks.

If West had the ♣A, there was no hope anyway. You can't win them all!

Key Point

When playing notrump, consider holding up your ace on the opening lead.

PROBLEM 9

You are South, declarer in 4♡.

```
              ♠  A Q 2
              ♡  10 9 7 6
              ◇  K Q 2
              ♣  J 4 3

                    N
                W       E
                    S

              ♠  4
              ♡  K Q J 8 5 4
              ◇  A J 4
              ♣  10 9 2
```

West	North	East	South
			1♡
pass	3♡	pass	4♡
all pass			

You have a minimum hand with a good heart suit, so you open 1♡. Partner raises you to 3♡, a limit raise showing 10-12 points and four hearts. The 6-4 trump fit improves your hand so you decide to have a go at game.

The lead is the ◇10. How do you plan to make ten tricks?

Analysis

Phew! You escaped a club lead. Your aggressive bid has landed you in a contract where you have three top club losers and you are also missing the ace of trumps.

How can you get rid of one of the club losers? Should you start by drawing trumps?

SOLUTION 9

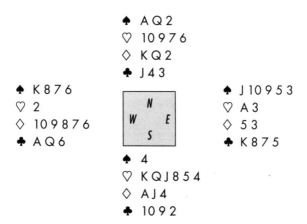

```
                    ♠ A Q 2
                    ♡ 10 9 7 6
                    ◇ K Q 2
                    ♣ J 4 3
   ♠ K 8 7 6                        ♠ J 10 9 5 3
   ♡ 2               ┌─────────┐    ♡ A 3
   ◇ 10 9 8 7 6      │    N    │    ◇ 5 3
   ♣ A Q 6        W  │         │ E  ♣ K 8 7 5
                     │    S    │
                    └─────────┘
                    ♠ 4
                    ♡ K Q J 8 5 4
                    ◇ A J 4
                    ♣ 10 9 2
```

You certainly cannot draw trumps immediately because the opponents can cash three club tricks when they get in with the ♡A.

There is only one way to eliminate a club loser and that is to discard it on a spade. So win the opening lead in your hand with the ◇J and lead the ♠4 towards dummy. West will play low so finesse the ♠Q from dummy. It wins, and you can then discard a club on the ♠A.

Now you can turn your attention to trumps and you will make your contract.

Key Point

Delay drawing trumps if necessary, in order to establish a winner in a side suit on which to discard a loser.

PROBLEM 10

You are East. After a simple bidding sequence, South is declarer in 3NT. Partner leads the ♣K.

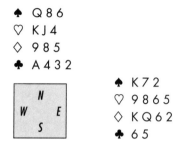

♠ Q 8 6
♡ K J 4
◇ 9 8 5
♣ A 4 3 2

♠ K 7 2
♡ 9 8 6 5
◇ K Q 6 2
♣ 6 5

West	North	East	South
	pass	pass	1NT
pass	3NT	all pass	

South opens 1NT (15-17 HCP). North has 10 HCP with no four-card major and goes straight to 3NT.

The lead is the ♣K, which declarer takes in dummy with the ♣A. Declarer now plays the ♠Q from dummy.

How do you play from here?

Analysis

Normally second hand plays low, but is that the case when an honor is led?

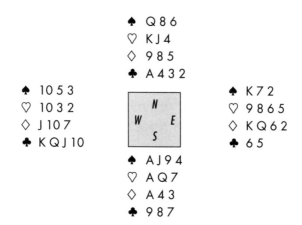

A good rule in defense is to cover a single honor led from dummy.

Look at what happens if you don't cover the ♠Q with your ♠K. The ♠Q wins the trick, then declarer leads the ♠6 from dummy and plays the ♠J. This wins and declarer continues with the ♠A, dropping your ♠K and establishing the ♠4 as a fourth trick in spades. Together with three tricks in hearts and the ◇A and ♣A, this ensures that the contract rolls home.

Now watch what happens when you cover the ♠Q with the ♠K. Declarer wins the ♠A and this promotes your partner's ♠10. Declarer can take the ♠J but the ♠10 will win the third trick in spades. What a huge difference this makes! Declarer can only take eight tricks — three spades, three hearts, one diamond and one club, and you will defeat the contract.

So remember the Golden Rule:

When dummy leads a single honor, cover it!

PROBLEM 11

You are South, declarer in 3NT.

```
              ♠ A 6 4
              ♡ A K 7 2
              ◇ 3 2
              ♣ 6 5 4 2

                   N
               W       E
                   S

              ♠ Q 5 2
              ♡ 5 3
              ◇ A 9 5 4
              ♣ A K Q J
```

West	North	East	South
			1NT
pass	2♣	pass	2◇
pass	3NT	all pass	

You have a balanced hand with 16 points, so you open 1NT. Your partner
bids 2♣ (the Stayman convention) to see whether you have a four-card major,
hoping that if you do it is hearts in which case 4♡ would be the best contract.
You reply 2◇ to deny a four-card major so partner bids game in notrump.

West leads the ◇K. How do you plan to play the hand?

Analysis

You count your winners — one spade, two hearts, one diamond and four
clubs. That's eight, so you need one more. The best chance for an extra
trick is a finesse in spades.

How do you proceed?

```
                    ♠ A 6 4
                    ♡ A K 7 2
                    ◊ 3 2
                    ♣ 6 5 4 2
 ♠ J 10 8                              ♠ K 9 7 3
 ♡ 10 9 6 4          ┌─────────┐      ♡ Q J 8
 ◊ K Q J 10         │    N     │      ◊ 8 7 6
 ♣ 9 7              │  W    E  │      ♣ 10 8 3
                    │    S     │
                    └─────────┘
                    ♠ Q 5 2
                    ♡ 5 3
                    ◊ A 9 5 4
                    ♣ A K Q J
```

It is good technique to hold up the ◊A for one round. In this case, you have six diamonds between your hand and dummy so if West has five of them, you only need to hold up once to exhaust diamonds in the East hand, so that East won't be able to return one on obtaining the lead. So you duck the opening lead and West continues with the ◊Q, which you win in hand with the ace.

Let's look at the spade suit. If West has the ♠K you could lead the ♠Q and try to finesse against it. But think about what happens when you lead the queen. West will cover it with the king and you will take it with the ace. Now you have no high cards left in spades! The point of finessing is to develop extra tricks but leading the queen hasn't achieved that. It is known in the trade as a 'no-win play'.

It is best to hope that East has the ♠K and you can make your queen by leading towards it. So play a heart to the ♡A in dummy and then lead the ♠4 from dummy. Whether East takes the ♠K or not, your ♠Q will become a winner.

The opponents can take the ♠K and three diamonds but you have nine tricks and your contract.

Key Point ────────────────────────────────

In general, lead towards your high card for a finesse.

PROBLEM 12

You are South. You are declarer in 4♠.

```
              ♠ K 5 4
              ♡ J 9 5 4 2
              ◊ K 6 5 2
              ♣ 5

                   N
               W       E
                   S

              ♠ A Q J 10 9 8
              ♡ A
              ◊ A 7 4
              ♣ 9 4 2
```

West	North	East	South
			1♠
pass	2♠	pass	3♠
pass	4♠	all pass	

You have a good hand with six spades and you open 1♠. North raises you to
2♠, you invite to game with your intermediate values, and North takes a rosy
view of the singleton club and bids 4♠.

The lead is the ♡K. Who has the ♡Q? How do you plan to play?

Analysis

West has almost certainly led from a sequence and thus has the ♡Q.

The first thing to do is to count your losers. You have none in
spades, none in hearts, one in diamonds and three in clubs — that's four,
one too many. How can you eliminate one of your losers? The hearts
look useless. If the diamonds are split 3-3 the thirteenth diamond will
become a winner, but it will be too late because the opponents will have
taken three club tricks by then. So the only possible suit for salvation
is clubs.

You can eliminate one or two club losers by ruffing them in dummy.
Are there any possible problems? Is there anything to stop you drawing
trumps at once and then leading a club?

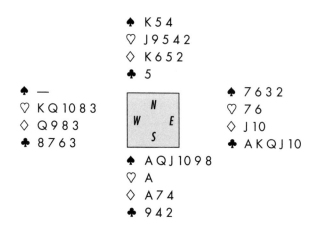

♠ K 5 4
♡ J 9 5 4 2
♢ K 6 5 2
♣ 5

♠ —
♡ K Q 10 8 3
♢ Q 9 8 3
♣ 8 7 6 3

♠ 7 6 3 2
♡ 7 6
♢ J 10
♣ A K Q J 10

♠ A Q J 10 9 8
♡ A
♢ A 7 4
♣ 9 4 2

You take the opening lead with the ♡A.

If you draw all the opponents' trumps immediately, there will be none left in dummy to ruff the clubs. The solution is to lead a club at Trick 2. East will win and probably lead a trump to shorten dummy's trumps. You take that with the ♠A and lead a second club and ruff it in dummy. Then return to your hand with a diamond to your ♢A and ruff the third club with the ♠K. Return to hand by leading a heart and trumping it with the ♠8. Draw the remaining trumps and you have eleven tricks.

In fact, you could afford to draw one round of trumps before leading a club. This would allow you to ruff one club in dummy and make ten tricks. But if you try to draw two rounds of trumps, West will lead a third one when in with the club winner and you are a goner.

Key Point

Delay drawing trumps if necessary, in order to ruff losers in dummy.

You are South, declarer in 4♠.

♠ A 7 5 4
♡ 9 8 7
◇ K 9 3
♣ K J 5

```
        N
    W       E
        S
```

♠ Q J 10 9 8 2
♡ 5 3 2
◇ A J
♣ A 7

West	North	East	South
	pass	pass	1♠
pass	3♠	pass	4♠
all pass			

You open 1♠ and North gives you a limit raise to 3♠, which shows 10-12 points and four spades. Your extra spade makes your hand better than a minimum and with ten trumps between you and your partner, you raise to game.

West leads the ♡A, then the ♡K. East plays the six then the four. Playing a high card followed by a low card is an encouraging signal to West, showing either the queen or a doubleton. In any case West can't go wrong by continuing with the ♡J. East takes it with the queen and switches to a diamond.

How do you plan to play the hand?

Analysis

You have already lost three tricks. There are no losers in clubs or diamonds but you must avoid a spade loser. You take the diamond switch with the ◇A in your hand.

Do you play the ♠A, hoping to drop the king, or do you lead the queen for a finesse, hoping that West has the king?

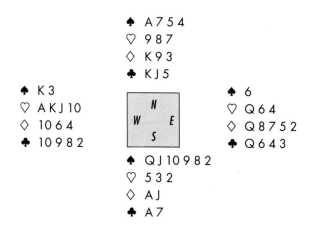

```
                    ♠ A 7 5 4
                    ♡ 9 8 7
                    ◇ K 9 3
                    ♣ K J 5
    ♠ K 3                              ♠ 6
    ♡ A K J 10          N              ♡ Q 6 4
    ◇ 10 6 4        W       E          ◇ Q 8 7 5 2
    ♣ 10 9 8 2          S              ♣ Q 6 4 3
                    ♠ Q J 10 9 8 2
                    ♡ 5 3 2
                    ◇ A J
                    ♣ A 7
```

Naturally, you lead the ♠Q from your hand hoping to see the king pop up from West. No such luck — West plays the three. What to do?

Playing the ace at this point will work in one case — when East has the singleton king. Playing low in dummy for a finesse will work in two cases — when East has the singleton six or a void. So it is definitely better to play for the finesse.

You don't have to work this out every time, just remember the key point:

Key Point

In a suit with ten cards, missing the king, it is best to take the finesse.

You are South playing in 3NT.

♠ 10 7 2
♡ A 8
♢ Q J 10 9 8 7
♣ 8 2

```
        N
   W         E
        S
```

♠ A J 6
♡ K 6 3
♢ A K
♣ A Q 7 4 3

West	North	East	South
			2NT
pass	3NT	all pass	

You have the hand of the session, a balanced 21 HCP, so you open 2NT and partner raises you to 3NT.

West leads the ♡Q. How do you plan to play the hand?

Analysis

In a notrump contract, the first thing to do is to count your winners. Things look quite rosy. You have one spade winner, two hearts, six diamonds and one club — that's a total of ten. Excellent!

Where should you start looking around for extra tricks? Are there any potential problems?

```
                    ♠ 10 7 2
                    ♡ A 8
                    ◇ Q J 10 9 8 7
                    ♣ 8 2
  ♠ Q 4 3                            ♠ K 9 8 5
  ♡ Q J 10 7 5      ┌─────────┐      ♡ 9 4 2
  ◇ 6 4 2          │    N    │      ◇ 5 3
  ♣ K 10           │ W     E │      ♣ J 9 6 5
                    │    S    │
                    └─────────┘
                    ♠ A J 6
                    ♡ K 6 3
                    ◇ A K
                    ♣ A Q 7 4 3
```

You need to be careful here. In order to take your six diamond tricks, you need to cash the ace and king in your hand first to unblock the suit. If you win with the ♡A in dummy at the first trick and then lead a diamond to unblock, you will never be able to return to dummy to enjoy the ◇QJ109!

You need to retain the ♡A in dummy as access to the diamonds. So win the opening lead in hand with the ♡K, cash the ◇A and ◇K and return to dummy with the ♡A. Then run the diamonds.

This way you will get your ten tricks.

Key Point

Keep a high card as an entry to the long suit.

PROBLEM 15

You are West. South is declarer in 3NT. You lead the ♡6.

```
                    ♠ A Q J 6
                    ♡ 8
                    ◇ K 10 9 4
                    ♣ 7 5 4 2
        ♠ 9 8 5         ┌─────────┐
        ♡ A J 9 6 3     │    N    │
        ◇ 6 3 2         │ W     E │
        ♣ Q 3           │    S    │
                        └─────────┘
```

West	North	East	South
			1NT
pass	2♣	pass	2◇
pass	3NT	all pass	

South opens 1NT (15-17 HCP) and North, who has four spades, bids 2♣ (the Stayman convention) to ask if South has a four-card major. South bids 2◇ to deny a four-card major and North, with enough strength for game, bids 3NT.

Your lead of the ♡6 is taken by East with the ♡K. East then plays the ♡2 to declarer's ♡10, which you capture with the ♡J.

How do you proceed?

Analysis

When returning partner's suit the standard method is to return your original fourth best if you started with four or more cards in the suit. Knowing this, how many hearts does declarer have left at this point?

What do you do now?

```
                    ♠ A Q J 6
                    ♡ 8
                    ◇ K 10 9 4
                    ♣ 7 5 4 2
    ♠ 9 8 5                         ♠ 10 7 4
    ♡ A J 9 6 3        N           ♡ K 7 4 2
    ◇ 6 3 2       W         E       ◇ 8 5
    ♣ Q 3             S            ♣ K J 10 6
                    ♠ K 3 2
                    ♡ Q 10 5
                    ◇ A Q J 7
                    ♣ A 9 8
```

It is a good thing in defense to get into the habit of counting declarer's cards.

When returning partner's suit you should play your highest remaining card if you started with three of them. If you started with four or more, return your original fourth best.

In the heart suit East returned the ♡2, which shows an original holding of four hearts. (It couldn't be only two cards because that would mean declarer had five — and declarer denied hearts in response to Stayman.) You had five hearts originally, dummy had one and partner had four. That is a total of ten so declarer started with three hearts, two of which have been played already. So that means declarer has just one remaining heart, the ♡Q in fact.

So you can confidently play your ♡A and drop declarer's ♡Q. Then you can play your ♡9 and ♡6. This gives you five heart tricks and the contract is defeated.

Key Point

When returning partner's suit, play the higher remaining card if you started with three cards in the suit. If you started with four or more, play your original fourth best.

PROBLEM 16

You are South, declarer in 1NT.

```
              ♠ K Q 4 3
              ♡ J 8 2
              ◇ 4 3 2
              ♣ 6 5 4

                   N
                 W   E
                   S

              ♠ 6 5 2
              ♡ Q 7 5
              ◇ A 10 5
              ♣ A K Q J
```

West	North	East	South
pass	pass	pass	1NT
all pass			

You have a balanced hand with 16 points, so you open 1NT and everyone passes.

West leads the ◇K. How do you plan to play the hand?

Analysis

You can count five winners — one diamond and four clubs. The best chance for two more tricks is the spade suit.

What spade layout do you hope for?

```
                          ♠ K Q 4 3
                          ♡ J 8 2
                          ◇ 4 3 2
                          ♣ 6 5 4
        ♠ A 8 7                              ♠ J 10 9
        ♡ 10 9 6 4         N                 ♡ A K 3
        ◇ K Q J 9      W       E             ◇ 8 7 6
        ♣ 9 7              S                 ♣ 10 8 3 2
                          ♠ 6 5 2
                          ♡ Q 7 5
                          ◇ A 10 5
                          ♣ A K Q J
```

You need to find the ♠A with West. In that case, if you lead twice towards the king and queen of spades in dummy they will each take a trick.

Normally you would duck the first round of diamonds, but a heart switch would not be welcome. So you take the opening lead in hand with the ◇A. Lead a small spade towards dummy. If West goes up with the ace you have two spade tricks. If West ducks, play the king from dummy. If it holds, don't play the queen but return to your hand in clubs and lead another spade towards the queen. The opponents can take the ♠A, three diamonds and two hearts but that is all, so you end up with seven tricks.

Don't just lay down your high honors to be taken by even higher ones — lead towards them. You need to hope that West has the ♠A. If East has it, *c'est la vie* - you probably cannot make seven tricks.

Don't lay down your high honors, lead towards them.

PROBLEM 17

You are South, declarer in 4♠.

```
              ♠  10 9 6 5 4
              ♡  8 2
              ◇  A K 4 2
              ♣  8 6

                    N
                W       E
                    S

              ♠  K Q J 8 7 2
              ♡  J 7 6
              ◇  Q 7
              ♣  A 10
```

West	North	East	South
			1♠
2♡	4♠	all pass	

You have 13 HCP and six spades, so you open 1♠. West overcalls 2♡. North has five-card support for your spades and decides that game is the place to be, and bids a simple 4♠.

West starts with the ♡A and ♡K, East following suit twice. West then switches to the ♣K.

How do you plan to play the hand?

Analysis

You have four losers — one in spades, two hearts already lost and one in clubs. The third heart loser in your hand can be ruffed in dummy later, so that is not a problem. But there is a loser in each of spades and clubs, so you need to eliminate one of them.

Any thoughts?

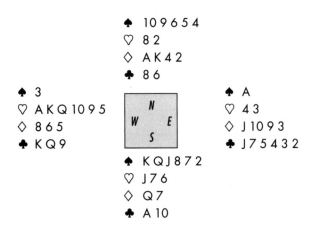

You win the club switch with the ace. Your club loser is now exposed to the wolves.

You should not play trumps immediately. If you do, the opponents will take their ♠A and then cash their ♣Q. The key is to play diamonds first. Play the ◇Q, then lead the seven to the ace in dummy and play the ◇K, discarding your club from hand.

Then you can afford to play trumps. The opponents will win the ♠A but you can ruff your remaining heart in dummy, making ten tricks.

Key Point

Delay drawing trumps if necessary, in order to discard losers on dummy's winners.

PROBLEM 18

You are South, declarer in 6NT.

```
          ♠ 8 2
          ♡ A Q
          ◇ A J 10 9 8
          ♣ A K 7 4

              N
          W       E
              S

          ♠ A K Q 3
          ♡ K 7
          ◇ 7 4 3
          ♣ Q J 9 8
```

West	North	East	South
			1NT
pass	6NT	all pass	

You have a balanced hand with 15 points, so you open 1NT. Partner has 18 points and, knowing that there are between 33 and 35 points in your two hands, bids a small slam.

The lead is the ♡J. How do you plan to play the hand?

Analysis

You have ten winners — three in spades, two in hearts, one in diamonds and four in clubs. The only possible source of extra tricks is the diamond suit.

How will you play the diamond suit?

```
                    ♠ 8 2
                    ♡ A Q
                    ◇ A J 10 9 8
                    ♣ A K 7 4
    ♠ 6 5 4                        ♠ J 10 9 7
    ♡ J 10 9 4 3 2    ┌─────────┐   ♡ 8 6 5
    ◇ Q 6 2           │    N    │   ◇ K 5
    ♣ 3               │ W     E │   ♣ 10 6 5 2
                      │    S    │
                      └─────────┘
                    ♠ A K Q 3
                    ♡ K 7
                    ◇ 7 4 3
                    ♣ Q J 9 8
```

You can only afford to lose one diamond trick. You could cash the ◇A and hope that either the ◇K or ◇Q is singleton, meaning you would only lose one trick to the other diamond honor. But this is a poor bet. The other approach is to play for West to have at least one of the missing diamond honors. Win the opening lead in hand with the ♡K and play a small diamond towards dummy. If West plays low, play the ◇J from dummy. Here this will lose to the ◇K and East will probably return a heart to your ace.

Return to your hand with a spade or a club and lead another small diamond towards dummy. If West plays low, play the ◇10 from dummy. It wins and East follows suit, so the queen is the only outstanding diamond and it will fall under the ace. Now you make four diamond tricks and your contract. The only way you would have failed is if the ◇K and ◇Q were both with East, which is only a 25% chance.

If East was unable to follow suit on the second diamond, this would tell you that West must have started with four diamonds to the queen. You would remain patient and return to your hand with a spade or club and finesse against the ◇Q again.

Key Point

When missing two honors in a suit, consider finessing twice. This technique is called a 'double finesse'.

PROBLEM 19

You are South, declarer in 3♣.

♠ 9 4 2
♡ K 3
♢ 9 5 4
♣ A K 8 7 3

♠ A K 7 3
♡ A 9 5 4
♢ Q 7
♣ 6 5 4

West	North	East	South
			1♣
pass	3♣	all pass	

You have 13 HCP and no five-card major, so you open 1♣, your longer minor. Partner has 10 points, no four-card major and five clubs, so gives you a limit raise to 3♣. This shows 10-12 points and usually at least five trumps. You have a minimum opening hand so you pass.

West leads the ♠Q.

How do you plan to play the hand?

Analysis ─────────────────────────────────

This hand looks different to most of the problems so far. What is the difference?

Normally the declarer has longer trumps than dummy. In this case you, South, have three trumps and dummy, North, has five. How does this affect your planning?

```
                        ♠ 9 4 2
                        ♡ K 3
                        ♢ 9 5 4
                        ♣ A K 8 7 3
      ♠ Q J 10 8                          ♠ 6 5
      ♡ 8 7 6         ┌─────────┐         ♡ Q J 10 2
      ♢ A K 10 2      │    N    │         ♢ J 8 6 3
      ♣ J 2           │ W     E │         ♣ Q 10 9
                      │    S    │
                      └─────────┘
                        ♠ A K 7 3
                        ♡ A 9 5 4
                        ♢ Q 7
                        ♣ 6 5 4
```

When counting losers, you look in the 'long hand', the hand with more trumps or, if they are the same length, the stronger trumps. So here you must count losers from the perspective of North: one loser in spades, three in diamonds and one in trumps if they split 3-2.

Can you eliminate one loser?

You can try to trump a diamond loser in the hand short in trumps, South. So win the lead with the ♠A in hand and, before drawing trumps, lead a diamond from your hand. Whoever wins this may lead a club to thwart your plan. Win the club with the ace and lead another diamond. If the defenders lead another club, win it with the king. Then lead dummy's last diamond and trump it in your hand.

You will eventually lose a trick to the ♣Q as well as a spade, but you will make your contract.

Key Point

Make sure you count losers in the 'long hand' — the one with more trumps.

You are East. South is declarer in 1NT. Partner leads the ♠2.

```
            ♠ Q 6 3
            ♡ K J 4
            ◇ 9 8 5
            ♣ A K J 2
                            ♠ A J 7
         ┌─────────┐        ♡ Q 8 6 5
         │    N    │        ◇ Q J 6
         │ W     E │        ♣ Q 6 5
         │    S    │
         └─────────┘
```

West	North	East	South
	1♣	pass	1NT
all pass			

North opens 1♣. South responds 1NT (6-9 HCP, no four-card suit outside clubs), ending the bidding.

Your partner leads the ♠2. Declarer calls for the ♠3 from dummy. How many spades does partner have? How many spades does declarer have?

How do you play?

Analysis

Partner is probably leading the fourth-best spade in which case they have four spades, and so South has three.

If there were three small spades in dummy, you would certainly play your ace. What do you do in this situation?

```
                    ♠ Q 6 3
                    ♡ K J 4
                    ◇ 9 8 5
                    ♣ A K J 2
    ♠ K 9 5 2                        ♠ A J 7
    ♡ 9 3 2          ┌─────────┐     ♡ Q 8 6 5
    ◇ K 10 7 2       │ W  N  E │     ◇ Q J 6
    ♣ 10 4           │    S    │     ♣ Q 6 5
                     └─────────┘
                    ♠ 10 8 4
                    ♡ A 10 7
                    ◇ A 4 3
                    ♣ 9 8 7 3
```

You should play the ♠J. The defense can now take four spade tricks. The
♠J wins, you cash your ♠A and return the ♠7 to partner's ♠K. The ♠9 now
takes the fourth trick. Your partner switches to diamonds and the contract
is defeated. If instead you take the ♠A at Trick 1, partner can take a trick
with the ♠K but declarer takes the third trick with the ♠Q in dummy. Then
declarer can play on clubs and make the contract.

You may well ask what would happen if declarer had the ♠K. Let's swap
the ♠K and the ♠10:

```
                    ♠ Q 6 3
    ♠ 10 9 5 2                        ♠ A J 7
                    ♠ K 8 4
```

If you play the ♠J, declarer takes it with the ♠K but later West can possibly
get in and lead the ♠10, trapping the ♠Q, in which case declarer makes only
one trick in the suit. If you play the ♠A, declarer is certain to take two tricks
with the ♠K and ♠Q.

So whether declarer has the ♠K or not, you come out even or ahead if
you play the ♠J at the first trick.

Key Point

*Retain an honor card over dummy's honor. Play your next highest card provided
it is a nine or better.*

PROBLEM 21

You are South playing in the popular contract of 3NT.

```
              ♠ K 6
              ♡ A 2
              ◇ Q J 8 4 3
              ♣ Q J 9 3

                 N
              W     E
                 S

              ♠ A 5
              ♡ K Q 4 3
              ◇ K 10 7
              ♣ K 10 7 5
```

West	North	East	South
			1NT
pass	3NT	all pass	

You open 1NT (15-17 HCP) and North, with no four-card major but enough points for game, raises you to 3NT.

West leads the ♠Q. How do you plan to play the hand?

Analysis ────────────────────────────────────

You have two tricks in spades and three in hearts, so you need to develop four more tricks.

Both diamonds and clubs offer good prospects for tricks. You have the king, queen, jack and ten in both suits. When developing tricks you normally choose the suit which has the most number of cards in the two hands. In this case you have eight cards in each suit.

Which suit do you attack?

```
                    ♠ K 6
                    ♡ A 2
                    ◊ Q J 8 4 3
                    ♣ Q J 9 3
    ♠ Q J 10 8 7 4      ┌──────────┐      ♠ 9 3 2
    ♡ 10 9              │    N     │      ♡ J 8 7 6 5
    ◊ A 2               │  W   E   │      ◊ 9 6 5
    ♣ A 8 2             │    S     │      ♣ 6 4
                        └──────────┘
                    ♠ A 5
                    ♡ K Q 4 3
                    ◊ K 10 7
                    ♣ K 10 7 5
```

There is an important difference between the diamond suit and the club suit. In clubs you have four cards in each hand whereas in diamonds you have five in one hand and three in the other. So by knocking out the ace you can develop four tricks in diamonds but only three in clubs. Since you need four more tricks for your contract, you must attack diamonds.

Note that there is not time to develop both suits. You have the ♠A and ♠K, one of which will win the first trick, and the defense will continue spades when they take their ◊A, so you will be exposed in spades after you win that trick. If you lose the lead again the opponents will take four spade tricks, so you cannot profitably knock out the ♣A as well as the ◊A.

Playing on diamonds, you take two spades, three hearts and four diamonds and make your contract.

Key Point

Establish the suit that will give you the greatest number of tricks.

PROBLEM 22

You are South, declarer in 3NT, yet again.

```
        ♠ K 5 4
        ♡ A 8 7
        ◇ K 9 3
        ♣ Q J 5 4

          N
      W       E
          S

        ♠ A 8 7
        ♡ K 5 2
        ◇ A 7 5 4
        ♣ A 7 3
```

West	North	East	South
			1NT
pass	3NT	all pass	

You have a very balanced hand with 15 points including three bullets. You open 1NT and partner, with no major suits but plenty of points, has no hesitation in raising you to 3NT.

West leads the ♠Q. How do you plan to play the hand?

Analysis

You have seven winners. Two more are needed from diamonds or clubs. You can make a long suit trick in diamonds if the suit breaks 3-3 but this is only a 36% chance. The club suit looks more promising.

You could try leading the ♣Q and finessing East for the king. Before you do, imagine how your hand and dummy would look if East had the king and covered the queen. You would take the ace and then the jack would also take a trick — but that comes to only eight tricks.

Is there anything else to try?

```
                    ♠ K 5 4
                    ♡ A 8 7
                    ◇ K 9 3
                    ♣ Q J 5 4
  ♠ Q J 10 9 2                      ♠ 6 3
  ♡ 10 6          ┌─────────┐       ♡ Q J 9 4 3
  ◇ 10 6          │    N    │       ◇ Q J 8 2
  ♣ K 10 9 2      │ W     E │       ♣ 8 6
                  │    S    │
                  └─────────┘
                    ♠ A 8 7
                    ♡ K 5 2
                    ◇ A 7 5 4
                    ♣ A 7 3
```

The best chance to make two extra tricks in clubs is to hope that *West* has the ♣K. If so, you can succeed by leading towards your queen and jack in dummy.

So win the first trick in your hand with the ♠A, play the ♣A (in case the king is singleton) then lead a small club towards dummy. If West plays the king, you play low in dummy and you immediately have two extra club tricks. If not, play the queen from dummy. If that wins, do not play the jack but return to your hand in hearts or diamonds and lead another small club towards the jack in dummy. This way, if West has the king, you make three club tricks.

Note that there is no point in hoping that East has the ♣K — you would only make three club tricks if the clubs were split 3-3, in which case it wouldn't matter how you played the suit.

 Key Point ───

In general, lead towards a high card for a finesse.

───

PROBLEM 23

You are South. You are declarer in 4♠.

♠ Q J 10 2
♡ 4 3 2
◇ 10 8
♣ K 8 6 2

```
      N
   W     E
      S
```

♠ A 9 6 5 4
♡ A J 6
◇ A K
♣ A 5 4

West	North	East	South
			2NT
pass	3♣	pass	3♠
pass	4♠	all pass	

You have a good balanced hand with 20 HCP and five spades so you open 2NT. North bids 3♣ (Stayman, just like over 1NT) and happily bids game when you show a spade suit.

The lead is the ♣Q. How do you plan to play the hand?

Analysis

The first thing to do is to count your losers. You have one in spades, two in hearts and one in clubs — that's four, one too many.

How can you eliminate one of your losers? The best chance is the trump suit. If East has the ♠K, you can finesse against it. That's a 50% chance, and if it doesn't come off, you might still find clubs 3-3.

How do you proceed?

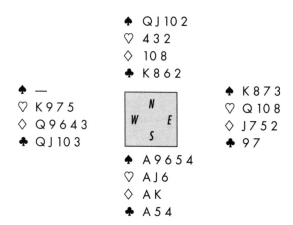

```
              ♠ Q J 10 2
              ♡ 4 3 2
              ◇ 10 8
              ♣ K 8 6 2
♠ —                          ♠ K 8 7 3
♡ K 9 7 5        N           ♡ Q 10 8
◇ Q 9 6 4 3   W     E        ◇ J 7 5 2
♣ Q J 10 3       S           ♣ 9 7
              ♠ A 9 6 5 4
              ♡ A J 6
              ◇ A K
              ♣ A 5 4
```

You need to win Trick 1 with the ♣K in dummy in order to lead spades through East. In general you should lead low for a finesse and if it works return in another suit and lead low again. That is out of the question here because there are no more entries to dummy!

You need to allow for the king to be protected by several small spades. If you have sufficient 'adjacent cards', it is acceptable to lead an honor for a finesse. In this case it is okay to lead the ♠Q because you have the jack, ten and nine as adjacent cards between your two hands.

So lead the ♠Q. If East does not cover with the king, play small from your hand and repeat the finesse by leading the ♠J from dummy to the next trick. If this is ducked, repeat it again by leading the ♠10. This way you will eventually pick up the king no matter how strongly it is guarded.

So you will lose only two hearts and one club, making your contract.

Key Point

Don't lead an honor for a finesse unless it is supported by at least one adjacent honor.

You are South, declarer in 4♡.

```
            ♠  J 6 3
            ♡  J 10
            ◇  A J 8 7 5
            ♣  A 5 3

                  N
               W     E
                  S

            ♠  7 4 2
            ♡  A K Q 9 7 3
            ◇  6
            ♣  K 9 4
```

West	North	East	South
			1♡
pass	2◇	pass	2♡
pass	3♡	pass	4♡
all pass			

You have a good hand with strong hearts and you open 1♡. North has five diamonds and 11 HCP and bids 2◇. You rebid your hearts, showing six of them. Your partner, encouraged by the ♡J10, invites to game and you bravely accept.

The lead is the ♣Q. How do you plan to play the hand?

Analysis

You have three losers in spades and one in clubs.

How can you eliminate one of your losers? There is no chance of ruffing one in dummy, so the only possible source of extra tricks is the diamond suit. How will you proceed?

```
                    ♠ J 6 3
                    ♡ J 10
                    ◇ A J 8 7 5
                    ♣ A 5 3
  ♠ Q 10                              ♠ A K 9 8 5
  ♡ 8 6 2          ┌──────────┐      ♡ 5 4
  ◇ K 9 2          │    N     │      ◇ Q 10 4 3
  ♣ Q J 10 7 2     │ W      E │      ♣ 8 6
                   │    S     │
                   └──────────┘
                    ♠ 7 4 2
                    ♡ A K Q 9 7 3
                    ◇ 6
                    ♣ K 9 4
```

To establish winners in the diamond suit you will need to play the ◇A and then trump three small diamonds in your hand. If the opponents' diamonds split 4-3, the fifth diamond in dummy will become a winner. This requires several entries to dummy: let's count them. You need to cross to dummy with the ◇A to ruff a diamond. You need to cross twice more to ruff diamonds and again after you draw trumps to cash the ◇J. That is three more entries after the ◇A. Do you have that many? If you take the opening lead with the ♣K in your hand, the ♣A will be an entry to dummy. Can you see two more entries to dummy?

Look at the heart suit. You have the ♡AKQ in your hand but the next two highest hearts are in dummy! So if you are careful, you can use the ♡J10 as entries. Take the ♣K in hand and start on the diamonds — play the ◇A then ruff a low diamond with the ♡3 in hand. Then play the ♡7 to the ♡J in dummy and ruff another diamond, not with the ♡9 but with the ♡Q. Why? You need to preserve the ♡9 to lead to the ♡10 in dummy in order to ruff another diamond — this time with the ♡K, which of course cannot be overruffed.

Whilst doing this you have drawn two rounds of trumps, both opponents following, fortunately. There is only one trump outstanding so draw it with the ♡A. Return to dummy via the ♣A and discard your remaining club on the established ◇J.

Key Point

Consider setting up extra tricks in a long suit in dummy by ruffing in your hand.

PROBLEM 25

You are East. South is declarer in 3NT. Partner leads the ♣K.

```
              ♠ Q J 8
              ♡ K J 4
              ◇ 6 5 2
              ♣ A 4 3 2
                              ♠ K 5 3
         ┌───────────┐        ♡ 9 8 6 5
         │     N     │        ◇ K 9 8 4
         │  W     E  │        ♣ 6 5
         │     S     │
         └───────────┘
```

West	North	East	South
	pass	pass	1NT
pass	3NT	all pass	

South opens 1NT (15-17 HCP). North has 11 HCP and no four-card major and bids 3NT.

Partner leads the ♣K. Declarer takes this in dummy with the ace and plays the ♠Q from dummy.

How do you play from here?

Analysis ───

If you play a low card, the queen wins and declarer continues with the jack. What do you do now?

```
                          ♠ Q J 8
                          ♡ K J 4
                          ◇ 6 5 2
                          ♣ A 4 3 2
        ♠ 10 6 2                            ♠ K 5 3
        ♡ 10 3 2          ┌─────────┐       ♡ 9 8 6 5
        ◇ Q 10 7          │    N    │       ◇ K 9 8 4
        ♣ K Q J 10        │ W     E │       ♣ 6 5
                          │    S    │
                          └─────────┘
                          ♠ A 9 7 4
                          ♡ A Q 7
                          ◇ A J 3
                          ♣ 9 8 7
```

A good rule in defense is to cover the last of touching honors led by dummy.

Look at what happens if you cover the ♠Q with your king. The ace wins the trick and declarer next leads the ♠4 from hand and plays the eight, finessing against your partner's ten. This wins and declarer continues with the ♠J, dropping your partner's ten and establishing the four as a fourth trick in spades. Together with three tricks in hearts and the ◇A and ♣A, this ensures the contract.

Now look at what happens when you don't cover the ♠Q with the king. If declarer continues with the ♠J you cover this time, declarer wins the ace and this promotes your partner's ten. Declarer can then develop a third spade trick by losing to partner's ten but that brings the total to only eight tricks — three spades, three hearts and one each in diamonds and clubs — and the contract is defeated.

So remember the Golden Rule:

 Key Point

When dummy leads touching honors, cover the last one!

PROBLEM 26

You are South, declarer in 3NT.

```
            ♠ 6 5 4
            ♡ A J 7 2
            ◇ 3 2
            ♣ A J 6 4

          N
        W   E
          S

            ♠ A K Q
            ♡ 5 3
            ◇ A 9 5 4
            ♣ Q 5 3 2
```

West	North	East	South
			1NT
pass	2♣	pass	2◇
pass	3NT	all pass	

You have a balanced hand with 15 points, so you open 1NT. Partner has 10 points with four hearts and bids 2♣ (Stayman). You have no four-card major so you bid 2◇ to show that, and partner jumps to game in notrump.

West leads the ◇K. How do you plan to play the hand?

Analysis

This is a very thin 3NT despite the combined 25 HCP between your hand and dummy. You have no useful spot cards and not a five-card suit to be seen. It's good that you like a challenge! You start with six tricks — three in spades, one in hearts, one in diamonds and one in clubs.

There are no more tricks available in spades and the chances of developing an extra heart or diamond trick are remote. The only realistic source of extra tricks is the club suit. You need to take a total of four tricks in clubs. If West has the ♣K, you can finesse against it.

What is the best way to do it? Should you lead the ♣Q?

SOLUTION 26

```
              ♠ 6 5 4
              ♡ A J 7 2
              ◇ 3 2
              ♣ A J 6 4
  ♠ 9 7 2                          ♠ J 10 8 3
  ♡ 10 9 6 4        N              ♡ K Q 8
  ◇ K Q J 10    W       E          ◇ 8 7 6
  ♣ K 8             S              ♣ 10 9 7
              ♠ A K Q
              ♡ 5 3
              ◇ A 9 5 4
              ♣ Q 5 3 2
```

First, win the opening lead with the ◇A in your hand. You decide not to hold up the ◇A because a heart switch would not be welcome.

Think about what will happen if you lead the ♣Q. West will cover it with the king. You can take the ace and then the jack will take the next trick but the opponents will be left with the ten, which will be high. You will have used two honors to capture one! It is a no-win play

Your only chance is that West has the doubleton ♣K. The correct line is to lead a small club from your hand and, if West plays low, finesse the jack from dummy. This wins and then you play the ♣A, felling the king! East follows suit so you now know that the suit is split 3-2. The queen then takes the third round and the opponents have no more, so you take four club tricks.

You were lucky that West had the doubleton ♣K, but that was your only hope. Sometimes dreams come true!

Key Point

In general, lead low for a finesse.

You are South, declarer in 3NT, your favorite contract.

```
        ♠  4 2
        ♡  A 7 5
        ◇  A J 9 5 2
        ♣  K 8 6
        ♠  A K 10
        ♡  4 2
        ◇  K 8 6
        ♣  A J 9 5 3
```

West	North	East	South
			1NT
pass	3NT	all pass	

You have a balanced hand with 15 HCP so you open 1NT. Partner, with 12 HCP and no four-card major, raises you to game.

West leads the ♡Q. How do you plan to take nine tricks?

Analysis

You have seven winners so you need to find two more. The diamond and club suits are possible sources of extra tricks. The queen is missing in both suits.

First of all you would like to exhaust one opponent of hearts, so you duck the opening lead. West continues with the ♡J which you also duck. East overtakes the ♡J with the ♡K and leads a third round of hearts, which you take in dummy with the ♡A, discarding the ♠10 from your hand. It seems that West led from a five-card suit and now East has no more hearts.

You now have a choice of finessing for the ◇Q or finessing for the ♣Q. Which finesse will you take?

SOLUTION 27

```
                    ♠ 4 2
                    ♡ A 7 5
                    ◇ A J 9 5 2
                    ♣ K 8 6
    ♠ Q J 3                         ♠ 9 8 7 6 5
    ♡ Q J 10 9 8        N           ♡ K 6 3
    ◇ 4 3           W       E       ◇ Q 10 7
    ♣ Q 10 7            S           ♣ 4 2
                    ♠ A K 10
                    ♡ 4 2
                    ◇ K 8 6
                    ♣ A J 9 5 3
```

This is a deal where you need to recognize the 'danger hand' and try to avoid giving that hand the lead. West's opening lead was a heart and it was probably from a five-card suit because East overtook the second round with the king to unblock the suit and then led a third round. If West has only four hearts you can afford to lose a trick to either hand, so assume the worst: West started with five hearts and has two winners ready to cash.

You must avoid taking a finesse that West could win, and so the way home is to finesse in diamonds, losing to East if necessary. So lead a small diamond to the ◇K in your hand then lead the ◇6 and play the ◇J from dummy. East will take a trick with the ◇Q but cannot hurt you because there is no choice but to lead a suit other than hearts. Fortunately, the diamonds are split 3-2 (which happens about two-thirds of the time), so you will take four diamond tricks, bringing your total to nine.

Key Point

Lose tricks to the safe hand.

PROBLEM 28

You are South, declarer in 4♡ after a competitive auction.

```
        ♠ A J 7 6
        ♡ A 9 8 6
        ◇ 4 3
        ♣ K Q 6

            N
        W       E
            S

        ♠ K 5 4
        ♡ K J 7 5 3
        ◇ A 9 5
        ♣ 10 7
```

West	North	East	South
3◇	dbl	pass	4♡
all pass			

West opens 3◇. This is a preemptive bid showing a hand with seven diamonds and less than an opening bid. Your partner doubles, showing a good opening hand with a shortage in diamonds and support for the other suits. You have close to an opening hand with five hearts, so you jump to 4♡, which becomes the final contract.

West leads the ◇K. How will you play the hand?

Analysis

You have one loser in spades, two in diamonds, one in clubs and a possible loser in hearts. One diamond loser can be ruffed in dummy so you would like to avoid losing a trick in trumps.

FIRST TRICKS

You win the ◇A in your hand, East following suit. There is no reason to postpone drawing trumps so you lead the ♡3 to the ace, both opponents following suit, and lead the ♡6 from dummy. East follows with the ten. Which card do you play from your hand — the king or the jack?

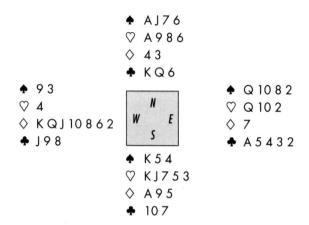

$\spadesuit$ A J 7 6
$\heartsuit$ A 9 8 6
$\diamondsuit$ 4 3
$\clubsuit$ K Q 6

$\spadesuit$ 9 3
$\heartsuit$ 4
$\diamondsuit$ K Q J 10 8 6 2
$\clubsuit$ J 9 8

$\spadesuit$ Q 10 8 2
$\heartsuit$ Q 10 2
$\diamondsuit$ 7
$\clubsuit$ A 5 4 3 2

$\spadesuit$ K 5 4
$\heartsuit$ K J 7 5 3
$\diamondsuit$ A 9 5
$\clubsuit$ 10 7

There is an old bridge adage: 'eight ever, nine never'. This means that with eight cards missing the queen you should always finesse but with nine cards you should play for the drop. Playing for the drop here means cashing the ace and then the king hoping that the queen will fall. The 'eight ever' part is generally true but the 'nine never' is a big exaggeration. With nine cards missing the queen the odds slightly favor the drop, but it is still close to even money.

Here you know that West started with seven diamonds and East must have started with only one. So East has much more room in his hand for the $\heartsuit$Q than West. Because of this you should assume that East has the $\heartsuit$Q and play the jack from your hand. The jack wins and you then draw the queen with the king.

Now you can lead a club from your hand towards the king and queen in dummy. If West has the ace (very unlikely after his preempt), you can discard your spade loser on a club. That doesn't work here, so try the spade finesse. Play the $\spadesuit$K, then lead a small one towards dummy and insert the jack. This also fails here but you are still able to ruff a diamond in dummy and make ten tricks.

Key Point

In a suit with nine cards missing the queen it is usual to play the ace and king, but the odds change dramatically after an opponent preempts in another suit.

You are South, declarer in good old 3NT.

```
              ♠  Q 7
              ♡  A K 5 3 2
              ◇  10 8 7
              ♣  7 4 3

                  N
              W       E
                  S

              ♠  A 3
              ♡  6
              ◇  A K Q 6 5
              ♣  A 10 9 6 5
```

West	North	East	South
		pass	1◇
pass	1♡	pass	3♣
pass	3◇	pass	3NT
all pass			

You have a strong hand with both minors, so you open 1◇, the higher of two five-card suits. Partner responds with 1♡ and you jump to 3♣ to show your strength. Partner gives diamond preference by bidding 3◇. You have a spade stopper so you try for the nine-trick game instead of 5◇.

West leads the ♡Q. How do you plan to play the hand?

Analysis

You count your winners — one spade, two hearts, three diamonds and one club. If the diamonds split 3-2 your small diamonds will become winners, making a total of nine.

Are there any problems?

```
                        ♠ Q 7
                        ♡ A K 5 3 2
                        ◇ 10 8 7
                        ♣ 7 4 3
     ♠ J 6 5 4                              ♠ K 10 9 8 2
     ♡ Q J 10 7      ┌─────────┐            ♡ 9 8 4
     ◇ J 3 2         │    N    │            ◇ 9 4
     ♣ Q 2           │ W     E │            ♣ K J 8
                     │    S    │
                     └─────────┘
                        ♠ A 3
                        ♡ 6
                        ◇ A K Q 6 5
                        ♣ A 10 9 6 5
```

You take the opening lead in dummy with the ♡A. The friendly split of the diamonds is your only real hope of making nine tricks. But if you play diamonds immediately you are doomed! You will no longer have access to the ♡K!

Once you realize there is a lack of entries to dummy, you will see that you have to cash the ♡K immediately and then start on the diamonds. They turn out to be friendly and you make your contract.

The chance of the 3-2 split when you hold eight cards in a suit is about 68%, which is a pretty good bet.

Key Point

Planning before you play to the first trick is vital.

PROBLEM 30

You are East. South is declarer in 3NT.

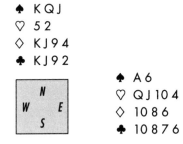

```
            ♠ K Q J
            ♡ 5 2
            ◇ K J 9 4
            ♣ K J 9 2
                        ♠ A 6
         N              ♡ Q J 10 4
       W   E            ◇ 10 8 6
         S              ♣ 10 8 7 6
```

West	North	East	South
		pass	1NT
pass	3NT	all pass	

Partner leads the ♠10. How do you plan the defense?

Analysis

A good thing to do as a defender is to count the high card points around the table. Declarer has 15-17 and dummy has 14, which is a lot. You have seven, so that does not leave much for partner. Partner has 2-4 points.

Declarer plays the ♠J from dummy and you take your ace. What should you do? Partners always like you to return their suit. Should you do that?

```
              ♠ K Q J
              ♡ 5 2
              ◇ K J 9 4
              ♣ K J 9 2
♠ 10 9 8 7 5                    ♠ A 6
♡ A 8 7 6        N             ♡ Q J 10 4
◇ 7 5 3      W       E         ◇ 10 8 6
♣ 5              S             ♣ 10 8 7 6
              ♠ 4 3 2
              ♡ K 9 3
              ◇ A Q 2
              ♣ A Q 4 3
```

The chances of defeating this contract are slim, but don't give up. Where can you get four more tricks from? There is not a lot of point in returning spades because dummy has the king and queen left. Is there any chance in another suit?

The only faint hope lies in the heart suit. You have to hope that declarer has the king and partner has the ace. So you switch to the ♡Q (top of a sequence). Declarer ducks and so does partner of course, and you continue with the jack. Declarer ducks again in the hope that West was dealt only two or three hearts to the ace. No such luck. You lead a third round and your side takes two more heart tricks. Declarer loses the ♠A and four hearts, mutters incoherently and vows to take up Poker instead of Bridge!

Key Point

Defenders, as well as declarer, need to plan at Trick 1.

You are South, declarer in 3NT.

```
            ♠ J 8 5 4
            ♡ 8 5 2
            ◇ K Q J 10 4
            ♣ K
```

```
              N
           W     E
              S
```

```
            ♠ A 6 2
            ♡ K 9 4 3
            ◇ A
            ♣ A Q 7 3 2
```

West	North	East	South
			1♣
pass	1◇	pass	1♡
pass	1♠	pass	2NT
pass	3NT	all pass	

You have a strong unbalanced hand with five clubs so you open 1♣. Your partner bids 1◇ and you bid your second suit, hearts. Partner then bids 1♠. It seems you don't have a fit anywhere so notrump may be the best spot. You bid 2NT, which is invitational to 3NT, and partner accepts the invitation.

West leads the ♡6. East takes the ♡A and returns the ♡J.

How do you plan to play the hand?

Analysis

Counting winners, you have one in spades, five in diamonds and three in clubs. With the heart opening lead, the king of hearts has also become a winner. That makes ten winners.

The diamond and club suits are blocked, so the challenge is to untangle your tricks.

How do you continue?

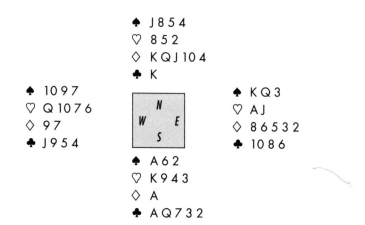

Before continuing it is critical to work out a sequence in which to take your tricks.

The diamonds in dummy are a source of tricks but the ace must be played from your hand first to unblock the suit. Similarly, to score the ♣A and ♣Q you need to unblock the king first.

The correct sequence is to take the ♡K, then the ◇A, then play a small club from your hand to the king in dummy. Then you cash the diamond honors in dummy, discarding two spades and two clubs from your hand. To enjoy the ♣A and ♣Q you need to come back to your hand, which you can do via the ♠A.

So you make ten tricks.

Key Point

Play high honors from the short side first to unblock a suit.

PROBLEM 32

You are South, declarer in only 1NT for a change.

```
        ♠  10 8 7
        ♡  9 3 2
        ◇  A K Q 7 6
        ♣  7 3

            N
        W       E
            S

        ♠  A 4 3
        ♡  A 8 7
        ◇  3 2
        ♣  A 6 5 4 2
```

West	North	East	South
			1♣
pass	1◇	pass	1NT
all pass			

You have a balanced hand with 12 HCP so you open 1♣. Partner with 9 HCP passes your 1NT rebid, which shows a minimum hand.

West leads the ♣K (anyway!).

How do you plan to take seven tricks?

Analysis

You have six winners so you need to find one more. From the opening lead it seems that clubs are not splitting 3-3, so the diamond suit is the only possible source of extra tricks. Note that there are no entries to dummy outside diamonds. That is a problem.

You can play the ◇AKQ, and if the diamonds split 3-3 you will make five diamond tricks and nine tricks in all. However if they do not split evenly you will only make three diamond tricks and six in all. The chance of a 3-3 split is only 36%.

Can you do better? How will you proceed?

SOLUTION 32

```
              ♠ 10 8 7
              ♡ 9 3 2
              ◇ A K Q 7 6
              ♣ 7 3
 ♠ K 9 2                        ♠ Q J 6 5
 ♡ 10 6 5 4      N             ♡ K Q J
 ◇ 8 4       W       E         ◇ J 10 9 5
 ♣ K Q J 10      S             ♣ 9 8
              ♠ A 4 3
              ♡ A 8 7
              ◇ 3 2
              ♣ A 6 5 4 2
```

The first thing to decide is whether to duck the first trick. It is normal to duck the first trick or two in notrump because West has probably led from a long suit, and in that case ducking will exhaust East in that suit. However, in this situation you should not duck, because they may switch to another suit in which you have fewer cards. In any case you can afford for clubs to be split 5-1.

So take the ♣A and then play on diamonds. The correct way is to play the ◇2 from your hand and the ◇6 from dummy. The opponents will win the trick but you will still have an entry to the remaining diamonds in dummy.

This way if the diamonds are split 3-3 or 4-2 you will make four diamond tricks and your contract. The chance that the diamonds are split 3-3 is 36% so if you are greedy and hope for that split you will be disappointed most of the time. The chance that the diamonds are split 4-2 is 48%, so the chance of a 3-3 or 4-2 split is 36% + 48% = 84%.

Here, the opponents will cash three club tricks when they win the first diamond but you will make your contract. If the diamonds were split 5-1 or 6-0 there was nothing you could have done about it anyway.

Key Point

Don't be afraid to give up a trick early. Sometimes it is the only way to make your contract.

PROBLEM 33

You are South, declarer in 7NT. Gulp!

$\spadesuit$ A K 8
$\heartsuit$ K 6 3
$\diamondsuit$ K Q 2
$\clubsuit$ A J 10 3

```
      N
   W     E
      S
```

$\spadesuit$ Q 7 6 2
$\heartsuit$ A Q 5
$\diamondsuit$ A J 4
$\clubsuit$ Q 6 4

West	North	East	South
		pass	1NT
pass	4♣	pass	4♠
pass	7NT	all pass	

You open 1NT. Partner, who has 20 HCP, should bid 5NT now, inviting you to bid 7NT with a maximum or sign off in 6NT — which with your poor 15 you would certainly do. However, partner has no intention of letting a potential grand slam slip away, and he bids 4♣, the Gerber convention, which asks how many aces you have. You reply 4♠ showing two aces, so partner goes all the way!

West leads the ♠J. You try to keep the horrified look off your face when you see dummy. How do you plan to play the hand?

Analysis

You have 35 HCP in total but neither hand has a five-card suit. You have ten tricks off the top — three spades, three hearts, three diamonds and one club. There are no extra red-suit tricks available so you look to spades and clubs. There is a small chance that the spades are split 3-3 but that would only give you one extra trick, so you need to work on the club suit. Assuming no help from the spade suit you need four club tricks. How will you play the club suit?

```
                    ♠ A K 8
                    ♡ K 6 3
                    ◇ K Q 2
                    ♣ A J 10 3
     ♠ J 10 9 5 3                      ♠ 4
     ♡ 9 2            N                ♡ J 10 8 7 4
     ◇ 8 7 5 3     W     E             ◇ 10 9 6
     ♣ K 5            S                ♣ 9 8 7 2
                    ♠ Q 7 6 2
                    ♡ A Q 5
                    ◇ A J 4
                    ♣ Q 6 4
```

You win the ♠A in dummy and cash the ♠K to test the spade suit in the vain hope that it splits 3-3. East shows out on the second round so you need to make four club tricks.

Obviously you need West to have the ♣K. It may seem intuitive to lead the ♣Q for a finesse. However, in the layout above West will cover with the ♣K and you will win in dummy with the ♣A. You can take the next two tricks with the ♣J and ♣10 but alas, East's ♣9 will now be the top club and you will only take three club tricks.

The correct play is to lead a low club from your hand towards dummy and insert the ♣J when West plays low. Then return to your hand and repeat the finesse by leading low towards dummy again. This time West will have to play the ♣K, which you will win with the ♣A. You will still have the ♣Q and the ♣10 as winners.

As a general rule it is preferable to lead a small card rather than an honor when finessing. This deal is a good illustration of the mechanism. In this situation, leading the ♣Q works only when the suit splits 3-3. Leading low works if West has ♣K, ♣Kx or ♣Kxx.

Key Point
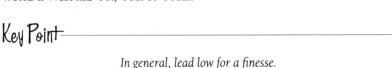

In general, lead low for a finesse.

PROBLEM 34

You are South, declarer in 3NT.

♠ A 4 2
♡ K J 10 9 8 2
◇ 6 5
♣ J 7

```
        N
    W       E
        S
```

♠ K 9 7 3
♡ Q
◇ K J 4 3
♣ A K 9 5

West	North	East	South
			1◇
pass	1♡	pass	1♠
pass	3♡	pass	3NT
all pass			

You have an unbalanced hand with 16 HCP and no four-card major, so you open 1◇. With four diamonds and four clubs it is usual to open 1◇. Partner responds 1♡ and you bid 1♠, still looking for a fit. Partner, with a good six-card heart suit, rebids 3♡, which is invitational to game. You have no heart support, but with the clubs well covered you bid 3NT.

West leads the ♣Q. How do you plan to play the hand?

Analysis

You only have four winners — two spades and two clubs, but you have five potential tricks in hearts once you knock out the ♡A.

It is best not to hold up a spade winner at Trick 1 because if the opponents find a diamond switch before you have set up the hearts, they might be able to cause you some trouble. You win the first trick in hand with the ♠K because you will need to preserve the ♠A in dummy to access the hearts.

How will you handle the hearts?

The Problems | 77 |

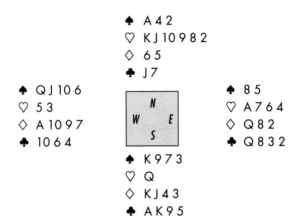

```
              ♠ A 4 2
              ♡ K J 10 9 8 2
              ◇ 6 5
              ♣ J 7
♠ Q J 10 6                      ♠ 8 5
♡ 5 3              N            ♡ A 7 6 4
◇ A 10 9 7    W       E         ◇ Q 8 2
♣ 10 6 4          S            ♣ Q 8 3 2
              ♠ K 9 7 3
              ♡ Q
              ◇ K J 4 3
              ♣ A K 9 5
```

If you play the ♡Q from your hand and a small heart from dummy and East takes the ♡A then you have no more problems — there are five heart winners in dummy that you can reach via the ♠A. But what happens if East ducks the ♡Q? Ducking the queen by holding up the ace would be the best play by East, who can see a total of ten hearts in the North and East hands, and deduces that South may have started with a singleton. In this case you will need to use up the ♠A entry in dummy in order to continue hearts to knock out the ♡A. Then after East takes the ♡A you will have no further entry to dummy.

The way to solve this dilemma is to overtake the ♡Q with the ♡K! Then it doesn't matter if East takes the ♡A immediately or not. You just keep leading out the hearts until East takes the ♡A. You still have the ♠A in dummy to access the hearts.

This should be part of the planning process at Trick 1.

Key Point

Be prepared to overtake an honor in order to preserve an entry.

PROBLEM 35

You are West. South is declarer in 3NT.

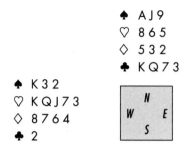

```
              ♠ A J 9
              ♡ 8 6 5
              ◇ 5 3 2
              ♣ K Q 7 3
  ♠ K 3 2          ┌─────────┐
  ♡ K Q J 7 3      │    N    │
  ◇ 8 7 6 4        │ W     E │
  ♣ 2              │    S    │
                   └─────────┘
```

West	North	East	South
			1NT
pass	3NT	all pass	

South opens 1NT (15-17 HCP) and North raises to game.

You lead the ♡K, the top of your sequence, and dummy comes down.

Declarer ducks the first heart, and you continue with the queen, which declarer takes in hand with the ace. Declarer now leads the ♣Q. Do you cover with the ♠K?

Analysis

Declarer would like to make three tricks in spades.

What do you do?

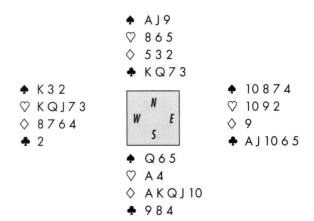

```
                ♠ A J 9
                ♡ 8 6 5
                ◇ 5 3 2
                ♣ K Q 7 3
   ♠ K 3 2                      ♠ 10 8 7 4
   ♡ K Q J 7 3      N           ♡ 10 9 2
   ◇ 8 7 6 4     W     E        ◇ 9
   ♣ 2              S           ♣ A J 10 6 5
                ♠ Q 6 5
                ♡ A 4
                ◇ A K Q J 10
                ♣ 9 8 4
```

Before you play to this trick, imagine what will happen if you cover or do not cover.

If you do not cover, declarer will play the nine from dummy. When the queen holds, another spade is certain to be led and, whether you play the king or not, the ace and jack in dummy will take two tricks. These three spade tricks would give declarer nine tricks, the contract.

If you cover the queen then the ace will win in dummy and the jack will be another winner. However, partner has the ♠10 and will have control of the third round of spades. Declarer may then switch to clubs but partner will take the ace, cash two spade winners and lead a heart to you. This will defeat the contract.

Note that you have to assume that partner has the ♠10, otherwise there is no hope. Certainly, not covering the ♠Q with the king is a losing play.

So remember the Golden Rule:

When declarer leads an honor, cover when there are two honors in dummy.

You are South, declarer in 4♠.

```
              ♠ Q 6
              ♡ Q 9 7 5
              ◊ Q 9 6 5 3
              ♣ 7 6

              ┌──────────┐
              │     N    │
              │ W      E │
              │     S    │
              └──────────┘

              ♠ A K J 10 3
              ♡ 4
              ◊ 7 2
              ♣ A K Q 9 5
```

West	North	East	South
			1♠
pass	1NT	pass	3♣
pass	3♠	pass	4♠
all pass			

You have 17 HCP and two good five-card suits, so you open 1♠, the higher suit. Partner scrapes up a 1NT response with 6 points and with your strong hand you jump the bidding to 3♣. Partner gives preference to your first suit by bidding 3♠ and you push on to game.

West leads the ♡J, which you duck in dummy. West wins the trick and continues with the ♡10, which you trump in your hand.

What is your plan?

Analysis

You have a loser in hearts, two in diamonds and also two in clubs. The first three are unavoidable so you need to do something about the club losers.

The club suit is different to many suits with losers in that you have most of the cards, seven, between your hand and dummy. It may be possible to establish a winner in the suit.

How will you handle the clubs?

```
                    ♠ Q 6
                    ♡ Q 9 7 5
                    ◇ Q 9 6 5 3
                    ♣ 7 6
     ♠ 4 2                          ♠ 9 8 7 5
     ♡ J 10 8 6          N          ♡ A K 3 2
     ◇ A J 10       W        E      ◇ K 8 4
     ♣ J 10 8 4          S          ♣ 3 2
                    ♠ A K J 10 3
                    ♡ 4
                    ◇ 7 2
                    ♣ A K Q 9 5
```

If the clubs are divided 3-3 in the opponents' hands, the suit is already established. Life is usually not that easy so you need a plan to cater for a 4-2 split. The chance of a 3-3 split is 36%, the chance of a 4-2 split is 48%.

The winning line is to cash the ♣A and ♣K and then ruff a small club with the ♠Q, which cannot be overruffed because you have all the higher trumps in your own hand. Because both opponents followed to the first two rounds, there is now only one club left, which will fall under the ♠Q, so the club suit is now established. You can lead the ♠6 from dummy, draw trumps and claim ten tricks. You used a trump in dummy to trump a loser and at the same time set up the rest of the club suit.

If clubs were split 5-1, an opponent would have trumped the second round of clubs and you would have gone down. Similarly, if trumps were split worse than 4-2, you wouldn't have made it either, but in these cases nothing would have helped. You can't win them all!

Key Point

A long suit in your hand can sometimes be established by ruffing in dummy.

You are South, declarer in 3NT.

♠ A Q 10
♡ 5
◇ Q J 10 9 6 5 3
♣ 8 5

♠ K J
♡ A K J 8 7
◇ 4
♣ A 10 9 4 2

West	North	East	South
		pass	1♡
pass	2◇	pass	3♣
pass	3◇	pass	3NT
all pass			

You open 1♡, the higher of your five-card suits. North has a good diamond suit and responds 2◇. You rebid 3♣, showing a better than minimum hand with a club suit. North repeats the diamonds; you have a spade stopper so you bid game in notrump.

West leads the ♣K. How will you play the hand?

Analysis

You have only six winners — three spades, two hearts and a club. The only way home is to set up the diamonds. You win the ♣A in your hand, East following suit, then lead the ◇4 to the ◇Q in dummy. East wins with the ◇A and returns the ♡10.

How do you play from here?

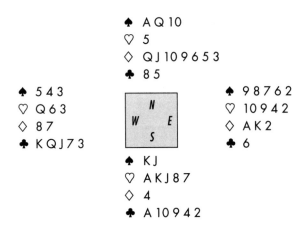

♠ A Q 10
♡ 5
◇ Q J 10 9 6 5 3
♣ 8 5

♠ 5 4 3
♡ Q 6 3
◇ 8 7
♣ K Q J 7 3

♠ 9 8 7 6 2
♡ 10 9 4 2
◇ A K 2
♣ 6

♠ K J
♡ A K J 8 7
◇ 4
♣ A 10 9 4 2

Take the ♡10 with the ♡A in your hand. You still need to drive out the ◇K and then return to dummy to enjoy the diamonds.

You have all the honors in spades but you must be careful to unblock so that you have two entries to dummy. If you lead the ♠J to the ♠A, you will never return to dummy.

So either play the ♠K to the ♠A in dummy or play the ♠J to the ♠Q in dummy. This will allow you to get back to dummy.

Lead the ◇J. If East ducks, continue with the ◇10. East will probably return another heart. Take the ♡K and return to dummy with a spade for the rest of the diamonds and the ♠10. You will end up with eleven tricks.

Key Point

Be prepared to overtake an honor in order to preserve an entry.

PROBLEM 38

You are South, declarer in 4♠.

♠ J 6 5
♡ 9 8 6
◇ 9 5
♣ 9 7 4 3 2

♠ A K Q 10 7 2
♡ A K 10
◇ K 7 4
♣ A

West	North	East	South
			2♣
pass	2◇	pass	2♠
pass	4♠	all pass	

You have 23 HCP and a strong spade suit, so you open 2♣, essentially forcing to game. Partner bids 2◇, a waiting bid that says nothing about diamonds. You show your spade suit by bidding 2♠. Partner has support for spades but nothing else and signs off in game.

West leads the ♣Q, which you win perforce with the ♣A in your hand. What is your plan?

Analysis

You have four losers - one in hearts and three in diamonds, so you need to eliminate one of them.

You could plan to ruff a diamond loser in dummy or you could play a diamond from dummy towards your ◇K. If East has the ◇A this will eliminate a diamond loser.

What will you do?

SOLUTION 38

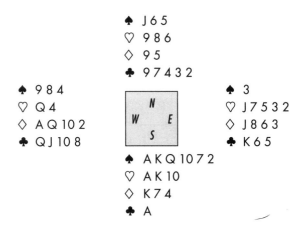

```
              ♠ J 6 5
              ♡ 9 8 6
              ◇ 9 5
              ♣ 9 7 4 3 2
  ♠ 9 8 4                      ♠ 3
  ♡ Q 4          N             ♡ J 7 5 3 2
  ◇ A Q 10 2   W   E           ◇ J 8 6 3
  ♣ Q J 10 8     S             ♣ K 6 5
              ♠ A K Q 10 7 2
              ♡ A K 10
              ◇ K 7 4
              ♣ A
```

Before proceeding, it is a good idea to play through both scenarios in your mind.

Let's mentally try leading a diamond from dummy towards the ◇K. The only way to dummy is to lead a spade to the ♠J. So you do that and lead a diamond from dummy. Let's assume the worst — West has the ◇A and returns a trump. You win and duck a diamond. West wins again and returns a third trump. This leaves you with no trumps in dummy to ruff a diamond, so you go down.

What happens if instead you duck a diamond immediately at Trick 2? The opponents can win and lead a trump but you then lead a second diamond. They can lead a second trump but you have the ♠J left in dummy to ruff the third diamond. This second plan will work, so it is the one to choose.

This is a case where South would have been better off being dealt the ◇2 instead of the ◇K. Then there would be no temptation to set up the ◇K.

Key Point

Ask yourself what could go wrong before deciding on a line of play.

You are South, declarer in 4♡.

```
        ♠ 9 5 4 2
        ♡ 7 6 2
        ◊ J 10 2
        ♣ A K 10

            N
        W       E
            S

        ♠ 6
        ♡ A K 9 5 4
        ◊ K Q 9 5 3
        ♣ Q 9
```

West	North	East	South
			1♡
pass	2♡	pass	3◊
pass	4♡	all pass	

You have 14 HCP and two good five-card suits, so you open 1♡, the higher suit. Partner, with 8 HCP and three hearts, gives you a single raise. You do not have quite enough to jump to game but you are strong enough to issue an invitation. You bid 3◊, continuing to describe your hand. Partner is at the top of his range with two top club honors and a little help in diamonds, so is happy to accept.

West leads the ♠K and continues with the ♠Q, which you trump in your hand.

What is your plan?

Analysis

There is one loser in spades, one in diamonds and one in hearts if they split 3-2.

You play the ♡A and ♡K, both opponents following suit. There is now only one trump outstanding, the queen.

Should you lead a third round of trumps to get rid of the queen?

```
                    ♠ 9 5 4 2
                    ♡ 7 6 2
                    ◊ J 10 2
                    ♣ A K 10
    ♠ K Q J 7                        ♠ A 10 8 3
    ♡ Q 10 3        ┌─────────┐      ♡ J 8
    ◊ A 7           │    N    │      ◊ 8 6 4
    ♣ J 5 4 2       │  W   E  │      ♣ 8 7 6 3
                    │    S    │
                    └─────────┘
                    ♠ 6
                    ♡ A K 9 5 4
                    ◊ K Q 9 5 3
                    ♣ Q 9
```

Your remaining trumps are ♡95 in your hand and ♡7 in dummy. If you lead another round West will take the queen and lead another spade. If you trump this you will be exhausted of trumps; now when you knock out the ◊A the opponents will take another spade trick and you will go down.

You should stop drawing trumps after two rounds and knock out the ◊A. As soon as the opponents take their ◊A, the rest of your diamonds are established. West can cash the ♡Q but you will still have a trump left and will make your contract.

In general it is not a good idea to draw the opponents' master trump unless you have a good reason, such as a long suit that you would like to run without interference. Here it would be downright dangerous.

Key Point

Do not draw the opponents' master trump unless you have a good reason.

PROBLEM 40

You are East. South is playing 3NT. Partner leads the ♡K.

```
                    ♠ 7 6 5
                    ♡ 7 6 2
                    ◇ J 10 7
                    ♣ A K Q 6
                                    ♠ J 3 2
              ┌─────────┐           ♡ A 3
              │    N    │           ◇ 9 8 6 5
              │ W     E │           ♣ 8 7 5 4
              │    S    │
              └─────────┘
```

West	North	East	South
	pass	pass	1NT
pass	3NT	all pass	

South opens 1NT and North, with 10 HCP and no four-card major suits, bids game in notrump.

West leads the ♡K.

Plan the defense.

Analysis

This is looking good. West is obviously leading from a sequence, either ♡KQJ or ♡KQ10 and you have the ♡A.

How should the play go from here?

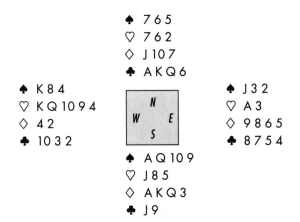

♠ 7 6 5
♡ 7 6 2
♢ J 10 7
♣ A K Q 6

♠ K 8 4
♡ K Q 10 9 4
♢ 4 2
♣ 10 3 2

♠ J 3 2
♡ A 3
♢ 9 8 6 5
♣ 8 7 5 4

♠ A Q 10 9
♡ J 8 5
♢ A K Q 3
♣ J 9

If you play the ♡3, you will have missed your opportunity for greatness. You can win the second round with the ♡A but there is no way back to partner's hand where all the good hearts are. Declarer will make nine tricks — a spade, four diamonds and four clubs.

You must overtake the ♡K with the ♡A and return the ♡3. That way your side will take the first five tricks in hearts and defeat the contract.

You know that partner has the ♡KQJ or ♡KQ10 so you can see how the play will pan out. It is an unblocking play that is available to defenders as well as declarers.

Key Point

Play high honors from the short side first to unblock a suit.

You are South, declarer in 2♠ for a change.

```
            ♠ Q 9 8 4
            ♡ A 8 3
            ◇ 10
            ♣ K Q J 10 9

              ┌─────────┐
              │    N    │
              │ W     E │
              │    S    │
              └─────────┘

            ♠ A K 7 6
            ♡ Q 6 5
            ◇ 7 5 4 3
            ♣ 6 3
```

West	North	East	South
	1♣	1♡	1♠
pass	2♠	all pass	

North opens 1♣ and East overcalls 1♡. You have 9 HCP and four spades, so you respond 1♠. Partner, with a minimum opening hand and four spades, raises to 2♠ and everyone passes.

West leads the ♡2.

What is your plan?

Analysis

You have two possible losers in hearts, four in diamonds and one in clubs. However, things are promising because three of your diamond losers can be ruffed in dummy and/or thrown on club winners.

East surely has the ♡K for the overcall so if you duck in dummy and East takes the ♡K, your ♡Q will be set up.

Is this the best way to proceed?

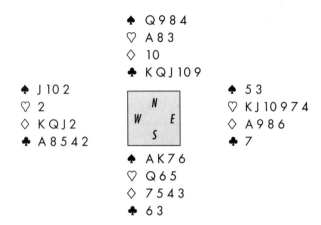

♠ Q 9 8 4
♡ A 8 3
◇ 10
♣ K Q J 10 9

♠ J 10 2
♡ 2
◇ K Q J 2
♣ A 8 5 4 2

♠ 5 3
♡ K J 10 9 7 4
◇ A 9 8 6
♣ 7

♠ A K 7 6
♡ Q 6 5
◇ 7 5 4 3
♣ 6 3

The lead of the ♡2 is ominous. A two is often the lowest card from four because the common lead from a long suit is the fourth highest. It may also be the lowest from a three-card suit containing an honor. It cannot be from a doubleton because the standard lead from a doubleton is the higher card. But here, because East has at least five hearts for the overcall, the ♡2 is clearly a singleton!

Look what happens if you duck the lead in dummy. East wins the ♡K and returns a heart, which West ruffs. West then leads a diamond to East's ace and East leads another heart, which West ruffs. Then West leads the ♣A and another club for East to ruff. You have just lost six tricks whilst watching helplessly from the sidelines. Your partner is looking equally stunned!

The sight of the ♡2 should ring alarm bells. You should immediately win with the ♡A, lead three rounds of trumps to deprive the defenders of their fun, and then play clubs until the defenders take their ♣A. When they do they may cash their ◇A, and possibly the ♡K, which will set up your ♡Q as a winner. In any case you will be able to dispose of three losers on the established clubs and ruff a diamond in dummy.

You will end up with only three losers. That gives you ten tricks instead of seven!

The opening lead of the two of a suit can be quite revealing.

PROBLEM 42

You are South, declarer in 3NT.

```
            ♠  10 7 2
            ♡  J 8 5
            ◇  A 10 8 7
            ♣  8 3 2

              N
           W     E
              S

            ♠  A K Q
            ♡  A K 2
            ◇  K J 6 4
            ♣  A 10 4
```

West	North	East	South
			2♣
pass	2◇	pass	2NT
pass	3NT	all pass	

You have been dealt a monster hand with 24 HCP so you open 2♣, your strongest bid. North responds with an artificial 2◇, waiting. You rebid 2NT showing a balanced 22-24 HCP. North happily raises you to game.

West leads the ♣K.

How do you plan to play the hand?

Analysis

You have eight top tricks — three spades, two hearts, two diamonds and a club. The diamond suit is the obvious candidate for an extra trick.

The clubs are a worry because you have only one stopper. So to get an idea of the distribution of clubs in the West and East hands, you should hold up your ace until the third round. East discards a spade on the third round of clubs. Aha! West started with five clubs and East with two.

How will you proceed?

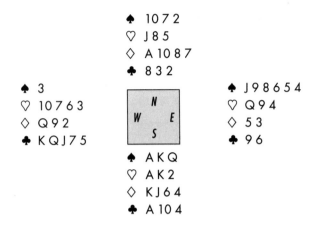

♠ 1072
♡ J 8 5
◇ A 10 8 7
♣ 8 3 2

♠ 3
♡ 10 7 6 3
◇ Q 9 2
♣ K Q J 7 5

♠ J 9 8 6 5 4
♡ Q 9 4
◇ 5 3
♣ 9 6

♠ A K Q
♡ A K 2
◇ K J 6 4
♣ A 10 4

It may feel normal at Trick 4 to play to the ◇A and then the seven to your jack to finesse against the queen, but that spells doom. West will take the ◇Q and cash two more club tricks.

Since you have the ◇10 as well as the jack, you can finesse either West or East for the queen. East is known to be out of clubs, so you should take the finesse in such a way that if it loses, East will be on lead and cannot continue clubs. So at Trick 4, play the ◇K and then the ◇4 to the ◇10 in dummy. Virtue is rewarded when the ten holds the trick and you make an overtrick.

You don't always have the luxury of a two-way finesse, but be aware of which is the danger hand.

 Key Point

Lose tricks to the safe hand if possible.

PROBLEM 43

You are South, declarer in 3NT.

```
        ♠ 10 9 8
        ♡ Q 9
        ◇ A K 10 8 6 4
        ♣ J 2

            N
        W       E
            S

        ♠ A K 4
        ♡ A 8 7 2
        ◇ 3 2
        ♣ K Q 4 3
```

West	North	East	South
			1NT
pass	3NT	all pass	

You have a balanced hand with 16 points, so you open 1NT. Partner has 10 points with a promising diamond suit and raises you to game.

The lead is the ♣7. How do you play the hand?

Analysis

The first thing to do is to count your winners. You have two in spades, one in hearts and two in diamonds — that's five, a long way from nine.

Two tricks can be developed in clubs but that is not enough. The source of salvation is the diamond suit. If the opponents' diamonds split 3-2 there are five tricks to be had. So you have to assume that they will split 3-2. However, if you play the ace, king and another first there will be no entry to dummy to enjoy the winners.

The answer is to lose a trick in diamonds first — that is, to duck the first round of diamonds in dummy. That way you retain an entry to dummy.

East plays the ♣10 on the opening lead and you win in your hand with the king. Now as per your plan, you play the ◇2. West plays the queen! This is unexpected. What do you do now?

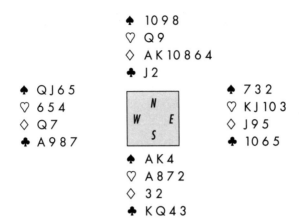

♠ 10 9 8
♡ Q 9
♢ A K 10 8 6 4
♣ J 2

♠ Q J 6 5
♡ 6 5 4
♢ Q 7
♣ A 9 8 7

♠ 7 3 2
♡ K J 10 3
♢ J 9 5
♣ 10 6 5

♠ A K 4
♡ A 8 7 2
♢ 3 2
♣ K Q 4 3

Do not be diverted from your quest! It is tempting to capture the queen with the ace but you had already determined that you cannot make the contract unless the diamonds split 3-2. So duck the diamond as planned! If you capture the queen, you will not make the contract.

It was extremely cunning of West to play the queen on the first round if diamonds. Most people would be fooled by it, but not you.

Key Point

Don't be afraid to give up a trick early. Sometimes it is the only way to make your contract.

PROBLEM 44

You are South, declarer in 4♡.

```
            ♠ Q 6 2
            ♡ Q J 6 3
            ◊ K Q J
            ♣ 9 8 6

              N
           W     E
              S

            ♠ A K 9
            ♡ 10 9 8 7 2
            ◊ 7 4
            ♣ A K 5
```

West	North	East	South
pass	pass	pass	1♡
pass	3♡	pass	4♡
all pass			

You have 14 HCP and a weak heart suit and open 1♡. North gives you a double raise to 3♡, showing 10-12 points and four-card trump support. Your heart suit has perked up with partner's support and you bid game.

West leads the ♣Q.

How do you plan to play the hand?

Analysis

Looking at losers, you have two in hearts and one each in diamonds and clubs. How can you get rid of one of them? There is nothing to trump in dummy, so you need to look at getting an extra trick from a side suit.

The diamond suit looks promising. Once the ace is knocked out you will have two tricks and could discard your club loser.

How do you go about the play?

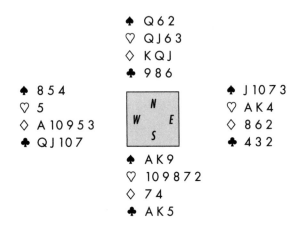

♠ Q 6 2
♡ Q J 6 3
◇ K Q J
♣ 9 8 6

♠ 8 5 4
♡ 5
◇ A 10 9 5 3
♣ Q J 10 7

♠ J 10 7 3
♡ A K 4
◇ 8 6 2
♣ 4 3 2

♠ A K 9
♡ 10 9 8 7 2
◇ 7 4
♣ A K 5

You win the club lead with the ace.

You should not play trumps immediately. If you do, the opponents will take their ♡A and then lead another club, which takes out your king and exposes the club loser. Then when you knock out the ◇A, they will cash their club winner.

The key is to play diamonds first so that you establish a diamond winner on which to discard your club loser. Play a small one from your hand to the king in dummy. If this is ducked by the opponents, continue with the queen. Whenever they take the ace, your jack is promoted to a winner. You then go to dummy, either by leading your remaining diamond if the ace was taken on the first round, or by leading a spade to the queen. Then discard the ♣5 on the high diamond in dummy. Now it is time to draw trumps.

The only tricks you lose are one diamond and two trumps, making your contract.

Key Point

Delay drawing trumps if necessary, in order to establish a winner in a side suit on which to discard a loser.

PROBLEM 45

You are East. South is playing 3NT.

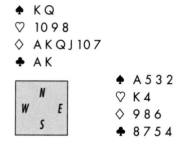

♠ K Q
♡ 10 9 8
◇ A K Q J 10 7
♣ A K

♠ A 5 3 2
♡ K 4
◇ 9 8 6
♣ 8 7 5 4

West	North	East	South
	2♣	pass	2◇
pass	3◇	pass	3NT
all pass			

North has a big hand with 22 HCP and opens 2♣. South responds 2◇ (waiting) and North shows his powerful diamonds. South is not interested, however, and North gives up any hope of slam and settles for game in 3NT.

West leads the ♠10 and declarer plays the ♠K, which you take with the ♠A. Partners generally like you to return their suit. Should you do this?

Analysis

Looking at dummy, things seem rather desperate. After you take the ♠A you can see that there are nine winners in dummy — one spade, six diamonds and two clubs. You would normally have considered holding up the ♠A with the ♠KQ in dummy, but not in this case.

Is there anything you can do?

SOLUTION 45

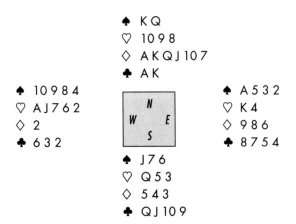

```
              ♠ K Q
              ♡ 10 9 8
              ◇ A K Q J 10 7
              ♣ A K
♠ 10 9 8 4                      ♠ A 5 3 2
♡ A J 7 6 2      N              ♡ K 4
◇ 2          W       E          ◇ 9 8 6
♣ 6 3 2          S              ♣ 8 7 5 4
              ♠ J 7 6
              ♡ Q 5 3
              ◇ 5 4 3
              ♣ Q J 10 9
```

There is only one suit that holds any promise for your side and that is hearts. If you return partner's suit or lead diamonds or clubs, you can see that declarer will rattle off nine tricks without raising a sweat. So hearts it is. Which card should you lead?

You must lead the ♡K! It is not very comfortable leading an unsupported king but look what happens if you lead the ♡4. If declarer plays the ♡Q, partner will win the ♡A and lead another heart to your ♡K, but you can't get back to partner's hand. If declarer instead plays a low heart, partner can win with the ♡J and play the ♡A capturing your ♡K but then declarer's ♡Q is high.

You must bite the bullet and play the ♡K. See how much easier it is now — the ♡K wins and you play the ♡4 and declarer's ♡Q is trapped. Partner takes four more heart tricks and the contract is defeated by two tricks.

It is true that if partner had led from that heart suit instead of safely playing the top of a sequence, your side could have wrapped up five quick heart tricks, but partners are not perfect and don't always make the best lead for a particular hand.

 Key Point

If there is only one way to defeat the contract, go for it!

PROBLEM 46

You are South, declarer in 6◇.

```
            ♠ A 5 3
            ♡ 7
            ◇ 10 9 7 2
            ♣ A J 8 4 3

                N
            W       E
                S

            ♠ 10 8 4 2
            ♡ A K Q
            ◇ K Q J 6 5 3
            ♣ —
```

West	North	East	South
			1◇
pass	2♣	pass	3◇
pass	4◇	pass	5◇
pass	6◇	all pass	

You have a hand with a lot of potential. You open 1◇ and partner bids 2♣.
You jump to 3◇ with your strong suit and partner raises to 4◇. You happily
bid game. Partner, with two aces, a singleton heart and good diamond
support, decides to put you in slam. Help!

West leads the ♠Q.

What is your plan?

Analysis ───

You have three losers in spades and the ace of trumps is out. One spade
can be discarded on the ♣A but that still leaves two more to be disposed
of.

You can't afford to draw trumps immediately because the spade
losers are exposed. This means the opponents could take their ◇A and
cash spades.

How will you proceed?

SOLUTION 46

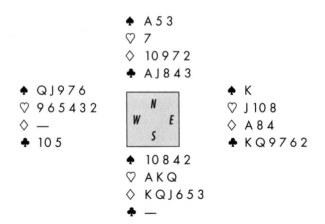

	♠ A 5 3 ♡ 7 ♢ 10 9 7 2 ♣ A J 8 4 3	
♠ Q J 9 7 6 ♡ 9 6 5 4 3 2 ♢ — ♣ 10 5	N W E S	♠ K ♡ J 10 8 ♢ A 8 4 ♣ K Q 9 7 6 2
	♠ 10 8 4 2 ♡ A K Q ♢ K Q J 6 5 3 ♣ —	

You take the opening lead with the ♠A, East following with the ♠K, which probably indicates a singleton.

The only way to dispose of the two spade losers is to ruff them in dummy. To prepare for this, play a heart from dummy to the ♡A in hand and then play the ♡K and ♡Q, discarding two spades from dummy. Now there are no spades left in dummy.

Now lead a small spade from your hand and ruff it in dummy. Because East played the ♠K on the first trick it is important to ruff high with the ♢10, which can only be overruffed by the ♢A. It would be a mistake to ruff with the ♢2 or the ♢7 because East would overruff with the ♢8.

If East does not overruff the ♢10, play the ♣A discarding a spade from your hand and lead a small club ruffing it in your hand. Then play another small spade and ruff it with the ♢9 in dummy. That's the end of the spades and the opponents will win the ♢A and nothing else.

If East does overruff the ♢10 with the ♢A, nothing can prevent you from ruffing another spade in dummy and discarding one on the ♣A.

Key Point

Delay drawing trumps if necessary, in order to ruff losers in dummy.

You are South, declarer in 4♡.

```
                    ♠ K Q 7 6
                    ♡ 9 8 6
                    ◇ A K 5 3
                    ♣ 3 2

                    ┌─────────┐
                    │    N    │
                    │  W   E  │
                    │    S    │
                    └─────────┘

                    ♠ J 2
                    ♡ A K 10 5 3
                    ◇ J 7 4
                    ♣ A 10 4
```

West	North	East	South
		pass	1♡
pass	1♠	pass	1NT
pass	4♡	all pass	

You have a minimum balanced hand with five hearts so you open 1♡, and after partner responds 1♠ you bid 1NT. Partner has an opening hand with three hearts and raises you to game.

West leads the ◇10.

What is your plan?

Analysis

You have one loser in spades, one in diamonds and two in clubs as well as one in hearts and only if they behave. A club loser can be ruffed in dummy so you need to eliminate one more.

What is the best way to proceed?

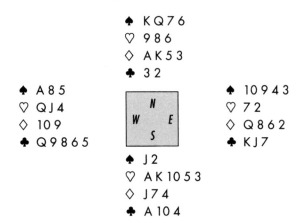

```
            ♠ K Q 7 6
            ♡ 9 8 6
            ◇ A K 5 3
            ♣ 3 2
♠ A 8 5                          ♠ 10 9 4 3
♡ Q J 4      N                   ♡ 7 2
◇ 10 9    W     E                ◇ Q 8 6 2
♣ Q 9 8 6 5      S               ♣ K J 7
            ♠ J 2
            ♡ A K 10 5 3
            ◇ J 7 4
            ♣ A 10 4
```

You should aim to knock out the ♠A and discard a diamond loser on the third round of spades. It is best to do this early because the opponents may lead another diamond when they get in.

Take the opening lead with the ◇A in dummy and lead a low spade to the ♠J in your hand. West will most likely win this with the ♠A and lead the ◇9, which you will take with the ◇K.

Now you can afford one round of trumps, so lead a small heart to the ♡A in your hand. Since you need to ruff a club in dummy later and you are going to have to lose the lead to achieve this, you cannot afford a second round of trumps. When the opponents get in they can lead a trump and you won't have one left in dummy to trump your club loser.

Next, lead the ♠2 to the ♠K in dummy and discard the ◇J on the ♠Q. That gets rid of your diamond loser. Now you can turn your attention to the club loser. Lead a small club from dummy to your ♣A and then duck a club. You can win any return and then ruff a club loser.

You will end up with only three losers — a spade, a heart and a club.

Key Point

Delay drawing trumps if necessary, in order to establish a winner in a side suit on which to discard a loser.

You are South, declarer in 4♠.

♠ A 6
♡ 8 7 5 4
♢ J 9 6
♣ A K 7 6

```
      N
   W     E
      S
```

♠ K Q J 10 9 3
♡ A K 2
♢ 7 3 2
♣ 9

West	North	East	South
	1♣	pass	1♠
pass	1NT	pass	4♠
all pass			

North opens 1♣ and you respond 1♠. North rebids 1NT, showing a balanced hand with 12-14 HCP. With your solid six-card spade suit, you have no hesitation in jumping to game.

West leads the ♣5. You win with the ♣A in dummy.

What is your plan?

Analysis

You have a loser in hearts and probably three losers in diamonds so you need to eliminate one. You note that a loser can be discarded on the ♣K. How will you proceed?

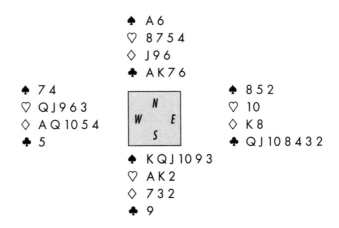

Entries to dummy are scarce so you need to choose the right time to take the discard on the ♣K. The temptation is to do it immediately, since the lead is in dummy when you win the ♣A. However, if you do that, West will ruff, and you will still have three more losers.

You can't draw all the opponents' trumps before you take the discard on the ♣K because you need at least three rounds of spades to do that. If you play more than two spades, you won't have an entry to dummy to cash the ♣K, but for maximum safety you should take two rounds to eliminate as many enemy trumps as possible. So lead a small spade to the ♠K in your hand then a small one from your hand to the ♠A in dummy. Both opponents follow, so there is only one trump at large. Now discard either a heart or a diamond on the ♣K. Fortunately, West has no more trumps and cannot ruff in. Now return to your hand by ruffing a club and draw the last trump.

It was unlucky that the clubs were split 7-1, but safe play saved the day.

Key Point

Draw trumps early unless you have a good reason for delay, such as trumping a loser in dummy or taking a discard.

PROBLEM 49

You are South, declarer in 3NT.

♠ A Q 10 8 7
♡ 6
◇ J 9 6 5 2
♣ A K

♠ 5 3
♡ A K Q
◇ 8 7 3
♣ Q J 10 9 8

West	North	East	South
		pass	1♣
pass	1♠	pass	1NT
pass	3◇	pass	3NT
all pass			

You have a balanced hand with 12 HCP so you open 1♣. Partner, with two five-card suits, responds 1♠, the higher one. You rebid 1NT with your minimum hand and partner jumps to 3◇ showing an opening hand and a diamond suit. You cannot support either of partner's suits, but you have hearts well and truly stopped so you bid 3NT.

West leads the ♡5, which you win in hand with the ♡A.

How do you plan to play the hand?

Analysis

You have six immediate winners — one spade, three hearts and two clubs. In fact, you have the top five clubs but once you play the ace and king there is no way back to your hand to cash the queen, jack and ten! Can you see any way of releasing the club suit from its bonds?

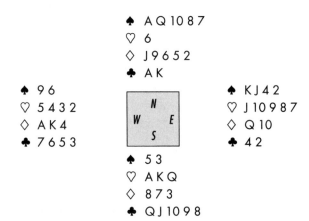

```
                    ♠ A Q 10 8 7
                    ♡ 6
                    ◇ J 9 6 5 2
                    ♣ A K
      ♠ 9 6                               ♠ K J 4 2
      ♡ 5 4 3 2          N                ♡ J 10 9 8 7
      ◇ A K 4        W       E            ◇ Q 10
      ♣ 7 6 5 3          S                ♣ 4 2
                    ♠ 5 3
                    ♡ A K Q
                    ◇ 8 7 3
                    ♣ Q J 10 9 8
```

If you could make the ♣A and ♣K disappear, the ♣QJ1098 could take five tricks, bringing your total to nine — five clubs, three hearts and a spade.

There is a way to make them disappear. Just discard them immediately on the ♡K and ♡Q!

It is so counter-intuitive to discard aces and kings that the solution is elusive, but it is really neat when you see it.

Key Point

Sometimes one suit can be used to unblock another.

PROBLEM 50

You are East. South is declarer in 5♣.

```
              ♠ 9 8 6
              ♡ K J 8 4 2
              ◇ 8 5
              ♣ Q 9 8
                              ♠ A 7 5 3
          ┌─────────┐         ♡ 5 3
          │    N    │         ◇ K Q 9 7 6
          │  W   E  │         ♣ A 7
          │    S    │
          └─────────┘
```

West	North	East	South
			1♣
1♠	2♣	4♠	5♣
all pass			

South opens 1♣ and West overcalls 1♠. North makes a single raise and you leap to 4♠. South buys the contract in 5♣. You think about doubling, but you're not sure who can make what, so you take a conservative view and pass.

Your partner leads the ♠K. How do you plan the defense?

Analysis ────────────────────────────────────

How many spades does partner have?

How many spade tricks can your side take?

What other sources of tricks are there?

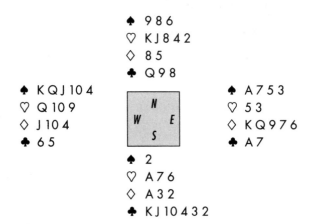

♠ 9 8 6
♡ K J 8 4 2
♢ 8 5
♣ Q 9 8

♠ K Q J 10 4   ♠ A 7 5 3
♡ Q 10 9   ♡ 5 3
♢ J 10 4   ♢ K Q 9 7 6
♣ 6 5   ♣ A 7

♠ 2
♡ A 7 6
♢ A 3 2
♣ K J 10 4 3 2

Partner has overcalled in spades, showing at least a five-card suit. With your four spades and dummy's three this leaves one spade for South at most, so your side cannot take more than one spade trick.

You will win a trick with the ♣A for sure. What other sources of tricks are there? You have the ♢KQ so you can probably set up a diamond trick while you still have the ♣A.

The key point here is that *you* know that a diamond switch is the right play, but partner may not! Partner may well continue spades at Trick 2, which could be disastrous. So you must take charge of the defense. Overtake partner's ♠K with your ♠A and switch to the ♢K and partner will love you forever. Well, until the next deal at least!

If the defenders don't switch to a diamond, declarer will make the contract by taking a heart finesse and then throwing the losing diamonds on dummy's long hearts.

 Key Point────────────────────────────────

Take charge of the defense when you can see the way home!

──

Standard Bidding System Used in the Problems

The bidding is mostly unimportant in the problems because generally the opponents do not enter the bidding, but it is discussed as a matter of interest.

This is the basic system used:

- An opening hand contains at least 11 HCP. Open a major suit if you have five or more cards in it, otherwise open your better minor.
  - ➤ With 3-3 in the minors, open 1♣.
  - ➤ With 4-4 in the minors, open 1◊.

- A 1NT opening bid is a balanced hand with 15-17 HCP.

- A 2NT opening bid is a balanced hand with 20-21 HCP.

- A single raise of an opening bid of a suit shows 6-9 points and at least three-card support.
  - ➤ For example:

    1♡ - 2♡

    1♠ - 2♠

- A double raise of an opening bid of a suit shows 10-12 points and four-card support. This is also known as a limit raise.
  - ➤ For example:

    1♡ - 3♡

    1♠ - 3♠

- A 2♣ opening shows a balanced hand with 22+ HCP or a game-forcing unbalanced hand. A 2◊ response is neutral ('waiting'), saying nothing about diamonds. A 2NT rebid by opener shows 22-24 HCP.

Stayman Convention

After partner opens 1NT, responder may use the Stayman convention to see if the partnership has a 4-4 fit in a major suit. With a 4-4 fit it is generally preferable to play in a major-suit contract rather than in notrump. This is how it works:

Responder bids 2♣. This says nothing about clubs, but asks if opener has a four-card major. Opener replies:

2◇ I have no four-card major (this says nothing about diamonds)
2♡ I have four hearts, and may also have four spades
2♠ I have four spades and do not have four hearts

If opener has a four-card major and it corresponds to responder's, the partnership will end up in a suit contract; otherwise, they will play in notrump. Responder needs at least 8 points to use the Stayman convention.

Glossary of Common Bridge Terms

Balanced hand	A hand with no void, no singleton and at most one doubleton.
Cover	Play a higher card on a card an opponent has led.
Danger hand	The opponent who, if on lead, can cash tricks or lead through your honors.
Develop	See *Establish*
Discard	The play of a non-trump when you cannot follow suit.
Duck	Play a low card when holding a higher one, and surrender a trick deliberately.
Entry	A card that can win a trick and thereby gain the lead for its holder.
Establish	Make your lower cards into winners by forcing out the opponents' higher cards in the suit.
Finesse	An attempt to take advantage of the favorable location of the opponents' cards, such as leading towards an ace-queen combination hoping that the king is onside.
HCP	High card points: A=4, K=3, Q=2, J=1.
Hold up	Delay the taking of a winner.
Long (trump) hand	The hand with more trumps than the other (usually declarer's rather than dummy's).
Major suit	Spades or hearts.
Minor suit	Diamonds or clubs.
Responder	The opening bidder's partner.
Ruff	The play of a trump on the lead of another suit.
Safe hand	The opponent's hand that is not the danger hand.
Sequence	A run of two or more consecutive honors.

Short (trump) hand	The hand with fewer trumps than the other (usually dummy's rather than declarer's).
Stopper	A holding that will prevent the opponents from immediately running tricks in a suit at notrump: examples are the ace or the king doubleton.
Unblock	Play or discard a high card that is preventing the run of a suit.

Problem Themes

Key Points

1. Develop tricks in suits where you hold more cards than the opponents.

2. Play high honors from the short side first to unblock a suit.

3. Where possible draw trumps before ruffing losers in dummy.

4. Develop tricks early while you still have stoppers in the other suits.

5. In defense when choosing a suit, lead through the strong hand and up to the weak hand.

6. Draw trumps early unless you have a good reason for delay, such as trumping a loser or taking a discard.

7. With eight cards in a suit missing the queen, finesse.

8. When playing notrump, consider holding up your ace on the opening lead.

9. Delay drawing trumps if necessary, in order to establish a winner in a side suit on which to discard a loser.

10. When dummy leads a single honor, cover it!

11. In general lead low for a finesse.

12. Delay drawing trumps if necessary, in order to ruff losers in dummy.

13. In a suit with ten cards missing the king it is best to take the finesse.

14. Keep a high card as an entry to the long suit.

15. When returning partner's suit, play the higher remaining card if you started with cards in the suit. If you started with four or more, play your original fourth best.

16. Lead towards honors.

17. Delay drawing trumps if necessary, in order to discard losers on dummy's winners.

18. When missing two honors in a suit, consider finessing twice. This technique is called a 'double finesse'.

19. Make sure you count losers in the 'long hand' — the one with more trumps.

20. Retain an honor card over dummy's honor. Play your next highest card provided it is a nine or better.

21. Establish the suit that gives the greatest number of tricks.

22. In general lead low for a finesse.

23. Don't lead an honor for a finesse unless it is supported by at least one more adjacent honor.

24. Consider setting up extra tricks in a long suit in dummy by ruffing in your hand.

25. When dummy leads touching honors, cover the last one!

26. In general lead low for a finesse.

27. Lose tricks to the safe hand.

28. In a suit with nine cards missing the queen it is usual to play the ace and king but the odds change dramatically after an opponent preempts in another suit.

29. Planning before you play to the first trick is vital.

30. Defenders need to plan at Trick 1 as well as declarer.

31. Play high honors from the short side first to unblock a suit.

32. Don't be afraid to give up a trick early. Sometimes it is the only way to make your contract.

33. In general lead low for a finesse.

34. Be prepared to overtake an honor in order to preserve an entry.

35. When declarer leads an honor, cover when there are two honors in dummy.

36. A long suit in your hand can sometimes be established by ruffing in dummy.

37. Be prepared to overtake an honor in order to preserve an entry.

38. Ask yourself what could go wrong before deciding on a line of play.

39. Do not draw the opponents' master trump unless you have a good reason.

40. Play high honors from the short side first to unblock a suit.

41. The opening lead of the two of a suit can be quite revealing.

42. Lose tricks to the safe hand.

43. Don't be afraid to give up a trick early. Sometimes it is the only way to make your contract.

44. Delay drawing trumps if necessary, in order to establish a winner in a side suit on which to discard a loser.

45. If there is only one way to defeat the contract, go for it!

46. Delay drawing trumps if necessary, in order to ruff losers in dummy.

47. Delay drawing trumps if necessary, in order to establish a winner in a side suit on which to discard a loser.

48. Draw trumps early unless you have a good reason for delay, such as trumping a loser or taking a discard.

49. Sometimes one suit can be used to unblock another.

50. Take charge of the defense when you can see the way home!

Master Point Press
on the Internet

www.masterpointpress.com

Our main site, with information about our books and
software, reviews and more.

www.teachbridge.com

Our site for bridge teachers and students — free downloadable
support material for our books, helpful articles and more.

www.bridgeblogging.com

Read and comment on regular articles from MPP authors and
other bridge notables.

www.ebooksbridge.com

Purchase downloadable electronic versions of MPP books
and software.